COLLECTOR'S EDITION

COLLECTOR'S EDITION

Innovative Packaging and Graphics

Stuart Tolley

Photography by Ivan Jones

481 illustrations

Thames & Hudson

HAND

Handmade, hand-manipulated and traditionally crafted
one-of-a-kind packaging and design

EXTRAS

Collectible memorabilia, ultimate collectors' editions and
sculptural objects incorporating digital technologies

INTRODUCTION /

Please: do not misinterpret this book. It is not anti-digital, and is certainly not intended to be a rehash of the digital-versus-print debate; in fact, some of the most innovative examples to be found in these pages combine both print and download technology to great effect. Rather, it is a celebration of beautiful design and specialist production. It sets out to showcase the new wave of large-format, limited-edition, handmade, lovingly produced objects being created for the music, book and magazine industries. It is about passion and connectivity between both the creators and the collectors. It is a conversation-starter.

A few years ago, the idea of a book celebrating the world of collectors' editions would not have seemed viable. Since 2008, when the most recent global financial crisis took hold, we have been living in uncertain times. The landscape in which we purchase music and the written word has changed beyond all recognition, with the market increasingly dominated by download and, most recently, streaming technology. The enormous popularity of MP3 players, tablets and e-readers has revolutionized the way in which we access new content. Indeed, digital downloads, e-books and online magazines were celebrated as the saviours of the music and publishing industries. At the same time, however, as budgets declined the days of vinyl records, hardback books, printed magazines and other tangible formats began to look numbered, and with them the opportunities for visual expression afforded by album sleeves, dust jackets and covers.

The demise of the physical format has been exacerbated by a change in shopping habits, with people favouring the convenience and cheaper prices offered by online retailers over independent record stores, news retailers and bookshops. According to British newspaper *The Independent*, for example, between 1998 and 2009 the number of independent record shops in the United Kingdom fell from 1,064 to just 269. This decline is passionately described in *Last Shop Standing* (2012), a film by Graham Jones based on his own book of the same name.

Without doubt, digital downloads and streaming are currently the most convenient and affordable ways to access new music and words. Downloads are immediate, practical and convenient, while a tablet or e-reader in your pocket makes paperback books and mainstream magazines look out of date. Even the easy access provided by downloads is being superseded by streaming technology, with such websites as Spotify reporting huge increases in user numbers.

However, as we enter a 'streaming era', in which ownership, format and quality become even less relevant – with streaming, you do not even possess a digital file – there has been a surprise renaissance in such traditional, higher-quality formats as vinyl, hardback books and beautifully produced magazines, especially in the area of independent publications aimed at niche markets. These often luxurious releases now sell faster than the standard formats of jewel-cased CDs, paperbacks and mass-market magazines – all of which have suffered the most at the hands of digital media.

There are a number of contributing factors to this renewed interest in the physical release. In the case of vinyl, which in recent years has seen a massive increase in sales, such events as Record Store Day – the international celebration of independent record shops that takes place every April – have helped to raise the profile of both vinyl itself and the small, independent outlets that sell it. Likewise, the burgeoning number of book and magazine fairs has highlighted the growth in independent publishing, exposing new markets and audiences to its wares. There has also been a resurgence in the use of traditional forms of manufacturing and production, including letterpress and screen printing, with a new generation of artists and designers shunning the computer screen in favour of getting their hands dirty.

Crucially, this renaissance in physical formats has contributed to a significant rise in the production of collectors' editions, the ultimate format for connecting artist and audience. Arguably, in the case of music, the shift from downloads to streaming has had the same effect, with people buying the collectible, special edition of an album to which they have been listening via a streaming site. But whatever the format, be it a limited-edition magazine with multiple cover options, a lavish box set of recorded music supplied with a wealth of extras, or a hardback book personalized by hand, collectors' editions are making their mark.

In our fast-paced lives, it comes as something of a relief to apply the brakes and enter the more expansive world of collectible physical formats. They offer

'The opportunities afforded by digital technology are undoubtedly exciting; equally compelling, however, is the rejuvenation of experimental print and production techniques. There is no reason why both technologies cannot coexist, and, as a result, create new and mould-breaking formats. Arguably, this is where the future of collectors' editions lies.'

us an opportunity to immerse ourselves in new ideas by means of sight and touch. Moreover, it is a world in which the people behind the scenes – the musicians, artists and collaborators – are returned to the spotlight.

The collector's edition, also known as the limited, deluxe or special edition, is not a new format. In the world of recorded music, box sets and gatefold LPs have been popular since the 1960s, in such diverse musical genres as big band, jazz, opera and rock. Released in 1964 by French singer-songwriter Léo Ferré, *Verlaine et Rimbaud chants par Léo Ferré* is regarded as the first double studio album. Limited-edition artist's books can be traced back to the late eighteenth century and the work of William Blake. While they were later popularized by William Morris and the Kelmscott Press in the 1890s, it was not until the 1950s and 1960s, with the release of books by artists Dieter Roth and Ed Ruscha, that the artist's book really took off.

The interest in and production of collectors' editions has risen dramatically since the late 2000s, among both small, independent companies and large multinationals. Pivotal to the rise of this new wave of tangible, specialist releases was the appearance in 2007 of the collector's edition of *In Rainbows* (see page 18),

British rock band Radiohead's seventh studio album. Released shortly after the groundbreaking 'pay what you want' digital download, the box set was initially the only physical manifestation of the record. Despite the relatively high price tag of £40, it was more than just an album: fans were also purchasing the artwork of Stanley Donwood, Radiohead's long-standing artistic collaborator. The *In Rainbows* box set is widely regarded as one of the most collectible of all contemporary music releases, with many people buying both it and the download.

While the range and variety of contemporary collectors' editions is considerable, it is possible to identify four key areas of interest. These areas, labelled 'Boxed', 'Multiples', 'Hand' and 'Extras', form the structure of this book. It is the first time that many of the featured items have been published together, and the intention was to focus on the innovative concepts that bind the artist and collector, as much as the beautiful design and production.

Traditionally, the format of choice for collectors' editions has been the limited-edition box set or boxed edition,

of which 'Boxed' contains numerous examples. In a larger size, such as the limited edition of *Mario Testino: Private View* (page 22), they often incorporate design features not found on the regular edition. Board is the most commonly used material, but as publishers experiment with new mediums and production techniques, the box set is evolving to include plastics, foam, metals and wood.

One way to create a desirable collector's edition is to release an edition with multiple cover options, as found in the 'Multiples' section. The buyer must then choose a preferred cover, a process that creates an implicit bond between them and the product. This technique has been successfully explored by the magazine industry, including *Wallpaper** (page 136), with a single issue featuring any number of cover options, thus adding to its 'shelf-ability'. However, the same technique has also been employed by record labels and book publishers, especially at the more lavish end of the spectrum. With the introduction of digital media, there are now more format options than ever before.

The handmade or hand-manipulated items in the 'Hand' section are intrinsically more desirable owing to their unique, 'one of a kind' nature. In each case, the artist has taken time to finish or modify the edition by hand, such as photographer Nadav Kander and his hand-painted book covers (page 192), thereby creating a personal connection with his or her audience. Hand-created editions can be tailor-made for an individual fan, and might contain personal messages. Although the widespread use of social media allows artists to speak directly to their audience, nothing can compare to a personalized hand-written message, something to be treasured.

Finally, the 'Extras' section looks at collectors' editions that come with additional memorabilia or other collectors' items. Such objects connect artist and audience by providing the fan with unique artefacts or limited-edition items that are unavailable in standard formats. In some cases, such as musician Peter Hook's book about the Haçienda nightclub (page 248), the extra objects are especially rare. When combined with digital media,

this exciting area of collectors' editions can create whole new platforms for creativity and expression, transforming traditional formats into works of sculpture. Extra items can also serve to enhance the original concept behind an object's creation, exploring new artistic avenues as a result.

All the items featured in *Collector's Edition* were photographed especially for the book – largely out of respect for the effort that has gone into making them. This level of detail, unusual for a publication of this kind, creates a uniform, neutral backdrop against which to explore and examine the work. Extended captions and production credits provide background information on each project.

A selection of exclusive interviews with leading practitioners provide valuable insights into the genre. Accompanied by specially commissioned portrait photographs, these interviews delve deeper into the decision-making behind key editions. It was important to provide a broad, balanced perspective on the creation and distribution of collectors' editions, which is why the interviews are with artists, musicians, designers, record labels and production experts.

In addition to showcasing the latest developments in specialist graphic design and packaging, this book has a practical element in the form of a list of production techniques and materials used in each project. These lists are designed to be flicked through, and provide a reference for those interested in a specific technique or material. Key production processes are also highlighted by the photography.

The opportunities afforded by digital technology are undoubtedly exciting; equally compelling, however, is the rejuvenation of experimental print and production techniques. There is no reason why both technologies cannot coexist, and, as a result, create new and mould-breaking formats. Arguably, this is where the future of collectors' editions lies. And, perhaps most importantly, it is the younger generation who are embracing this future. Having grown up with and become used to digital technology, they are now beginning to discover the rewarding world of printed media. It is this understanding of both worlds that provides exciting opportunities for a new generation of designers.

While downloads and streaming remain the most popular and convenient means of consuming new content, such mid-range, uninspiring and uncollectible formats as jewel-cased CDs, paperback books and mainstream magazines are on the wane. On the rise are collectors' editions: beautiful objects created in limited numbers and, in many cases, accompanied by a digital version. Imbued with love, skill and passion, they offer a chance to experience radical and innovative concepts in packaging and design in parallel to digital technology. These are, in fact, exciting times.

BOXED

Box sets, boxed editions, large-format packaging and limited-edition collectibles

Radiohead
Haruki Murakami
Orchestral Manoeuvres in the Dark
Mario Testino
Stroboscopic Artefacts
Alan Moore & Mitch Jenkins
Bonobo
mono.kultur
Silversun Pickups
Shout Out Louds
Erased Tapes
Eleh
Stéphanie Solinas
Gustav Mahler
Squarepusher
The Horrors
Fiona Tan

Kishi Bashi
Slanted
Popol Vuh
The Clarke & Ware Experiment
Jennifer Butler & Irma Boom
Arve Henriksen
Can
DJ Shadow
Mumford & Sons
Julian Sartorius
Oasis
Autechre
My Wet Calvin
Amon Tobin
The Breeders
Air
The National
Edgar Martins
:zoviet*france:
Warp
Die Schachtel
Russian Criminal Tattoo
WassinkLundgren
Muse

STANLEY

DONWOOD

INTERVIEW : MATTHEW LEE

PHOTOGRAPH : IVAN JONES

STANLEY DONWOOD is best known for his work with Radiohead, with whom he's collaborated since 1994. In addition to creating artwork for seven albums, numerous singles, EPs and DVDs, and side projects by band members Thom Yorke and Jonny Greenwood, Donwood has published books of art and short fiction, had his work exhibited worldwide, and briefly run a record label.

In 2009 Donwood won a Grammy Award for his work on the collector's edition of *In Rainbows* (2007; see page 18), an album that was pivotal in changing the way we think about music distribution. Radiohead 'leaked' the album through their website, bypassing a record label and allowing fans to pay what they wanted. The collector's edition of the album came out shortly after the 'leak date', followed by a standard CD. It was the first time that a major band had chosen a pay-what-you-want distribution model for a new album, and it was a major success: download sales netted Radiohead almost $3 million.

Was there a sense of extra pressure creating artwork for the collector's edition of *In Rainbows* when the music was legally available for free?
I was speechless when Thom told me I had to make something worth £40. It took me a while to get my head around it, so it took a lot of time. There were a lot of mock-ups.

How did you form the idea for the *In Rainbows* artwork?
The idea I ended up going with wasn't my original idea. I'd been inspired by James Howard Kunstler's book *The Long Emergency*, which is about a future without oil. It made me think of these alienated landscapes, acres and acres of car parks with shopping malls condensed into cathedrals, and lots of little houses occupied by people who are alive only to consume. But when I heard the music, it was organic, sexual, sensual and very human, and this idea didn't seem suitable.

Where did you create this work?
The band recorded *In Rainbows* in Savernake Forest in Wiltshire, in an incredible stately home called Tottenham House. I worked alongside them throughout the whole process. The house is like Buckingham Palace reimagined by J. G. Ballard. There's an outdoor swimming pool with green water, and there was a dead deer floating in it. The place became increasingly decrepit as you ventured further upstairs. There were baths full of dead flies and dead birds. There was also a crazy hidden door in a hidden library, and if you went through it and up the stairs you ended up in the quarters where 'mad' King George III stayed when he thought he was being poisoned at court in London. His marble bath takes up the whole room, and it was full of dead insects – absolutely disgusting.

How long were you there for?
About a month. We couldn't stay in the house, so the band were in caravans out back and I stayed in my teepee. By the end of October, it had got a bit cold. I thought the canvas of a teepee was waterproof, but on the last day we had this horizontal rain, and my living arrangements didn't end up being very luxurious. There was a huge hole in the middle of the house. The roof leaked, so it was flooded. There was only one functioning toilet, and you had to step across paving stones to reach it. We used the one serviceable wing of the house to build the studio.

Did this environment have an impact on your work?
I'm not sure. It probably did, but these things are intangible. I recall Thom getting quite ill, but Nigel [Godrich, Radiohead's producer] loved it and has very fond memories.

What inspired the work with the hypodermic needles?
I was working in the old school room, full of these great big church candles. I accidentally spilled a load of wax on something I was drawing, and that became the germ of the final artwork, using wax and hypodermic needles. A doctor friend supplied me with lots of needles with sharps on them. You can use them like a fountain pen while slowly pressing on them. Because we're not machines, you occasionally get this little 'spasm' of ink, which you don't get with a pencil. It's as if you're drawing in this weird, injured way, so the drawing has an un-human element. Around the time I started becoming interested in ink and velocity and what happens when ink hits a surface hard, I was on a train travelling with a paintball gun, which looks just like a gun, as well as a whole load of hypodermic needles. All these police got on the train, and I thought, 'God, if I get caught, how will I explain this one?'

Is it normal for you to work while the band are making the album?
Yes, but since I don't know anything about music, I just hear them playing the same bloody thing over and over again. To an untutored ear such as mine, it all sounds the same.

You also used Photoshop for the *In Rainbows* artwork. How long has software played a part in your art?
I started using Photoshop in 1994 for *My Iron Lung*, the first record I did with the band. We'd bought a computer. It cost about seven and a half grand, and was probably far less powerful than an iPhone, and we did all those things people do when they first use Photoshop and get excited by the filters. You'd do things randomly, and sometimes it would be really ugly and other times it would work. I've never properly learned how to use Photoshop. I'm a total luddite. My children think it's hilarious that I've been using computers for as long as I have, but I've yet to master relatively simple things, such as having a contacts list in my email. A lot of it is just boring. However, when we started working together the Internet was very exciting. While making *OK Computer* [1997] we created the first Radiohead website in SimpleText. Your options are limited when you're working on a 14.4 modem.

In those days CDs were still king …
I fucking hate CDs. I really don't like them. Those clattery boxes, those jewel cases they come in. The middle bit always breaks. In terms of art, there are a limited number of things you can do with a CD. And with that record, it was only their third album, and you'd have to argue with the record company over everything, every page in the booklet.

Has Radiohead's success given you greater creative freedom?

Definitely. It went from 'what's wrong with a single folded bit of paper?' to 'what do you want to do for the special edition this time?', and we'd start being taken out for nice meals so we could talk about the feasibility, for example, of turning *Hail to the Thief* [2003] into a giant map that folds out like an Ordnance Survey map.

The collector's edition for *The King of Limbs* [2011; see page 232] is very different from the one for its predecessor, *In Rainbows* ...

The idea was for the music to outlive the packaging by a significant margin. You could have killed someone with the *In Rainbows* limited edition if you'd hit them hard enough, but *TKOL* is just newsprint, really shit quality. I was reading the newspaper outside on a sunny day, and I left it on my seat for a few hours and when I returned it had started to crinkle up and turn yellow. I wanted to make something so terrible that just by opening the packaging it starts to degrade. It mirrors our own decay, the way we become more wrinkly. It's a collector's edition you can't collect. It came in plastic packaging that you had to destroy just to reach the music. And I managed to find a type of plastic that degrades in sunlight, so it's almost impossible to keep it in mint condition, unless it's kept in a vault. It was a reaction to the coffee-table glossiness of *In Rainbows*. My main inspiration was selling something that self-destructs. There's a famous Durutti Column LP. The sleeve is made of sandpaper, so every time you put it in your record collection it fucks up all the others.

Why did you start your own record label [the short-lived Six Inch Records]?

I was drunk. It was around Christmas, and I was really quite pissed. I've always envied people who have hobbies, such as keeping model trains or something, and I thought I'd be a record company boss, just for fun. So I emailed various musicians I know with this great idea and proposed a deal: we put out records, they get half, I get half, and it'll be great. It was a bit more work than I was expecting. We released only three records, in an edition of 333 each time, and each record was priced at £6.66. It wasn't a good business model, but we made a couple of hundred quid. And by the time of the label launch party we'd sold out, so I sacked all my artistes and took voluntary redundancy.

Is there also nostalgia for newsprint and newspapers in this work?

Definitely – I can't deny it. *The Universal Sigh*, the free newspaper Radiohead made for *The King of Limbs*, was amazing. I felt like a Bond villain as it all came together. Even XL [the record label that released the physical editions of the album] needed convincing. Why put out a newspaper that doesn't even mention the band or the name of the record? But it got in all the real newspapers, and since it's newsprint it was really cheap to produce. It was at the height of the free newspaper thing, and I thought it was amazing how everybody took a paper and read it.

The Universal Sigh was handed out to commuters in more then fifty cities worldwide. As your art begins to reach an increasingly global audience, do you feel a greater level of responsibility in terms of its meaning or message?

I think I'm aware that I may exercise a little more caution than I did when I was twenty-five and didn't care. Lately, the art has seemed to be less political, both in terms of what I've done and in terms of what the band has done. I used to believe very strongly that the purpose of art was to raise people's awareness of issues I felt were important. It's a very solipsistic point of view to hold.

Were both you and the band angrier in the early days?

Yes, of course. It's common among men in their twenties. There was a compatibility with the band. We're all the same age, but it's a long time ago, and now we're more mellow. I can't really remember what we were angry about. Although I still get cross sometimes, and I do political work under an assumed name.

'You could have killed someone with the *In Rainbows* limited edition if you'd hit them hard enough, but *The King of Limbs* is just newsprint, really shit quality.'

Stanley Donwood is a pen name, not your real name. Are you and Stanley Donwood the same person?

No, we're not. I first started calling myself Stanley Donwood to separate the person doing the artwork from the new father who was going to playgroups and changing nappies. Everybody has different personas that they inhabit, and it's just an exaggeration of that. When I work under different names, I inhabit different characters. One of my favourite personas is a guy called Lexton Morant, an antiquarian ghost-hunter and publisher.

You've also worked on Thom Yorke's solo project, and with his new band, Atoms For Peace. Is the process different from working with Radiohead?

Yeah, it's different. With Radiohead there's five in the band and five creative influences that have to be meshed together, so that's a fancy construction, a complicated edifice. Atoms For Peace feels more straightforward. It feels like we're a gang – me, Thom and Nigel [Godrich] – and we go out to the US to see Flea, Joey [Waronker] and Mauro [Refosco, the other members of the band]. I've been around for the recording of both *The Eraser* [2006, Yorke's solo album] and *Amok* [2013, the debut album by Atoms for Peace; see page 104], and the artwork for these records is a continuation.

What inspired the artwork for these records?

I was in Cornwall in 2004 and there was a big flood. It was terrifying. I had this book of woodcuts from the Nuremberg Chronicle [a medieval history of the world], and I was copying them, all the waves and the flooding, and that became *The Eraser*. I really like linocuts. I love the crudeness of them. The woodcuts in the Nuremberg Chronicle are really bad, even for the fifteenth century. The cover art for *The Eraser* was part of an exhibition of my work called 'London Views' [2006]. I didn't go out and look at the places in London being flooded. I did it from memory, and I did it badly on purpose.

Do you feel your career is defined by your work with Radiohead?

It would be weird if I didn't think that was the case. It works because I'm interested in what they're doing, and they're interested in what I'm doing. When I'm working on their records, and my artwork reaches a certain point, they put it on all the screensavers in the studio and I get loads of feedback from them. I'd go crazy if I had to work on my own all the time. Twenty years in my studio on my own and I'd have gone totally insane. I'm not very good at being alone.

Are you with Radiohead for the long haul?

Yeah, I'm there for as long as Radiohead's around.

What would you be doing now if you hadn't met Thom Yorke at art college?

I have no idea. I was unemployed when Thom called and said, 'Do you want to have a go at doing a record cover?' and I said, 'Alright', and that was *My Iron Lung*. I'd probably have had to get a job. I'm temperamentally unsuited to getting up early and going to an office.

Is it really true that you were working as a fire-breather when you first met the band?

Yes. If you don't mind having breath that smells of paraffin, it's really quite easy. You don't need any skills, and people are really impressed and say, 'Wow, look at that. Let's give him 2p.'

Will visual art continue to be an important part of music?

It is and it always has been. As a kid I'd buy records on the strength of the cover. In record shops I was too scared to go into the booth and listen to something on headphones, so I'd buy records on the basis of their covers. And often it would work out. I heard loads of good stuff because of good artwork. When I was really young, perhaps twelve years old, I got into Tubeway Army. I remember getting my mum's greaseproof paper and tracing the artwork on the album sleeve, and I think somewhere I've still got that record with all the dents in the cardboard where I traced it with a pencil. Artwork is part of the music – it's all entwined.

Stanley Donwood was photographed at his studio in Bath, UK

Radiohead
In Rainbows

◇◇◇◇◇◇◇◇◇◇◇◇◇◇◇◇

Specifications
2 180gsm 12" vinyl records
2 CDs
Booklet
Casebound slip case
Die cutting
Folding board
Hardback book
Matt lamination
Matt UV varnish
Rigid board
Thread sewing
Wire stitching

The release of Radiohead's seventh studio album was announced on the band's website. 'Well,' the message began, 'the new album is finished, and it's coming out in ten days ... We've called it *In Rainbows*.' Significantly, it was initially available as a download only, for which fans could pay what they want; a selection of physical releases came later. Created by Stanley Donwood, the deluxe limited-edition box set has become a highly collectible item, providing inspiration for a new generation of lavish music packaging. In 2009 *In Rainbows* won two Grammy awards: one for Best Alternative Music Album, and the other for Best Boxed or Special Limited Edition Package.

—

PUBLISHER *Radiohead, UK*
ART DIRECTION & DESIGN
Stanley Donwood
PRODUCTION *Clear Sound & Vision*
DATE *2007*

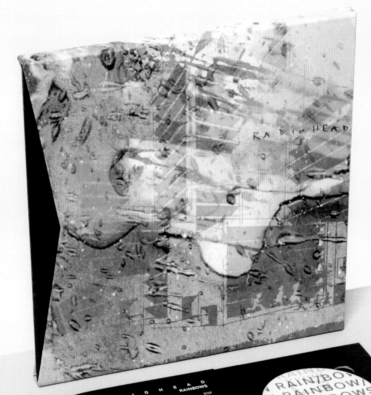

Haruki Murakami
1Q84

✕✕✕✕✕✕✕✕✕✕✕✕✕✕✕✕✕✕✕✕✕✕✕✕✕✕✕✕✕✕✕✕✕✕✕✕✕✕

Specifications
2-colour offset printing
3 paperback books
Acetate
Matt UV varnish
Slip case

This three-volume paperback edition of Haruki Murakami's bestselling novel *1Q84* (see also page 204) was the creation of Vintage and Anchor Books art director John Gall. The books are designed to be visible through a clear plastic slip case featuring wraparound typography.
—

PUBLISHER *Vintage Books, USA*
ART DIRECTION & DESIGN *John Gall*
DATE *2012*

Orchestral Manoeuvres in the Dark
English Electric

English Electric is the twelfth studio album by Orchestral Manoeuvres in the Dark (OMD), one of the leading exponents of British new wave in the late 1970s and early to mid-1980s. The record is also the band's second album since their reformation in 2006, having split a decade earlier.

OMD vocalist and bass player Andy McCluskey knew that he wanted the release of *English Electric* to have a collector's element. The band's rich visual history certainly had a bearing on the project's outcome. The result saw a distillation of many ideas into the simplest of solutions: a

matt-black tin containing such colourful and varied content as a blue 7" record and a selection of art and photographic prints.

—

PUBLISHER *100% Records, UK*
CREATIVE DIRECTOR *Tom Skipp*
ILLUSTRATION *Tom Skipp*
PRODUCTION *Modo*
DATE *2013*

Specifications
2 CDs
4 art prints
4 photographic prints
Blue 7" vinyl record
Booklet
Debossing
DVD
Flood coating
Gloss lamination
Hand-signed
Lift-off-lid tin
Matt lamination

Mario Testino
Private View

◇◇◇◇◇◇◇◇◇◇◇◇◇◇◇◇◇◇◇

Specifications
Black acrylic
Book cloth
Foil stamping
Hand finishing
Hand-signed
Hardback book
High-gloss resin varnish
Injection-moulded plastic
Lenticular cover
Plastic case
Spot UV varnish
Edition of 1,500

Published to coincide with the first exhibition of his work to be held in China, *Mario Testino: Private View* is a selection of the Peruvian-born photographer's fashion and celebrity images. Available in pink, purple or green, this limited edition was produced in Taschen's 'XL' format (45 × 33.5 cm/17¾ × 13¼ in.), with an inlaid lenticular cover photograph of Lady Gaga. All material choices were made in collaboration with Testino, who personally signed every copy of the limited edition. The highly sculptural high-gloss presentation case features the book's title in both Roman script and Chinese characters.

—

PUBLISHER *TASCHEN, Germany*
ART DIRECTION & DESIGN
Higher and Higher
PHOTOGRAPHY *Mario Testino*
PRODUCTION *Javier Bone-Carbone, Toppan Leefung*
DATE *2012*

MARIO TESTINO PRIVATE VIEW 私視角

TASCHEN

Stroboscopic Artefacts
Stellate 4

◇◇◇◇◇◇◇◇◇◇◇◇◇◇◇◇◇◇◇◇◇

Specifications
2 transparent 10" vinyl records
Aluminium
Art print
Hand-numbered
Lift-off-lid tin
Edition of 300

Stellate 4 is the fourth and final release in Stroboscopic Artefacts' Stellate Series, which brings together the work of sixteen different experimental music producers. In common with the first three releases, *Stellate 4* includes a hand-numbered inlay by Palermo-based art collective Oblivious Artefacts; placed together, the inlays from all four releases form one complete design. Separating the two 10" records is a typographic print on recycled paper.

—

PUBLISHER *Stroboscopic Artefacts, Germany*
ART DIRECTION & DESIGN
Luca Mortellaro, Ignazio Mortellaro, Marco Morici (Oblivious Artefacts)
DATE *2013*

Alan Moore & Mitch Jenkins
Unearthing

◇◇◇◇◇◇◇◇◇◇◇◇◇◇◇◇◇◇

Specifications
1 white 12" vinyl record
2 black 12" vinyl records
3 CDs
Dot matrix printing
Hardback book
Photographic print
Poster
Printed transcript
Slip case
Spot gloss UV varnish
Suspended wallets

The *Unearthing* box set is the culmination of a literary and photographic project between writer Alan Moore and photographer Mitch Jenkins, based on a story of the same name by Moore. The box set contains all the work created for the project, including the audio version of *Unearthing*, the accompanying soundtrack and a printed transcript of the story.

—

PUBLISHER *Lex Records, UK*
ART DIRECTION *Paul Chessell,*
Mitch Jenkins, Lex Records
DESIGN *Paul Chessell*
PHOTOGRAPHY *Mitch Jenkins*
ILLUSTRATION *Steve Moore*
PRODUCTION *Clear Sound & Vision*
DATE *2010*

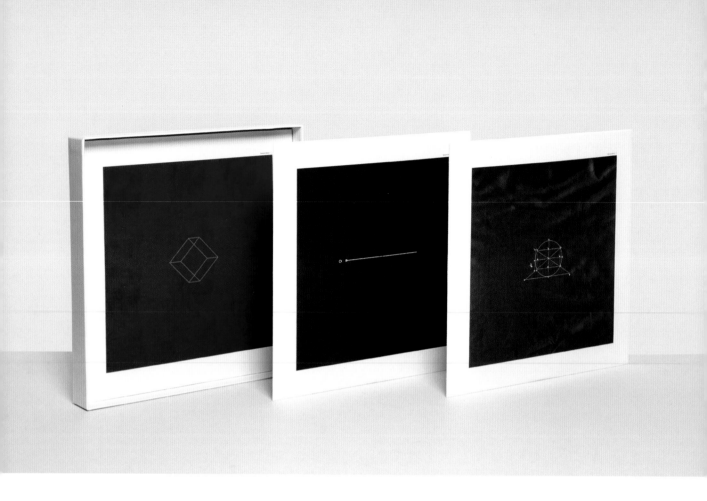

Bonobo
The North Borders

Specifications
3 posters
7 10" vinyl records
CD
Lift-off-lid box
Matt lamination
Matt UV varnish
Red satin ribbon
Rigid board

Sean Preston of Ninja Tune comments that achieving the high quality for which the record label is known was central to the making of this box set. The whole package had to match the quality of not only the recorded content, Bonobo's fifth studio album, but also the beauty of designer Leif Podhajsky's rich imagery.

Producing the vinyl was the most time-consuming task. Ninja Tune pressed thirteen sides on to a total of 28,000 vinyl discs, and etched on to the N-side (the back of the seventh disc). One concern was that 10" discs can feel flimsy,

but pressing them at a heavier weight can result in issues with sound. The label's usual plant had to be persuaded to increase the grammage, but they persevered, and the test pressings sounded spot on. The heavier vinyl fits in well with the whole box, which Preston was keen to keep as thick and weighty as possible. The lift-off-lid box is made of rigid board, and a thick matt paper coats it. The sleeves are 300 gsm double whiteboard, as is the case with all the label's 12" releases.

The red ribbon is an especially nice touch, allowing fingernail-

preserving access to the posters, the vinyl and the CD. While the use of coloured ribbon is not an original idea, in this context it works very well. Many box sets look anything but premium, but here every detail has been considered; in fact, it's the way in which the whole package fits together so neatly that is particularly satisfying.

—

PUBLISHER *Ninja Tune, UK*
ART DIRECTION *Leif Podhajsky, Ninja Tune*
DESIGN *Leif Podhajsky*
ILLUSTRATION *Leif Podhajsky*
PRODUCTION *Sean Preston*
DATE *2013*

mono.kultur
mono.archiv #02

XXXXXXXXXXXXXXXXXXXXXXX

Specifications
15 issues of magazine
Cardboard
Hand-assembled box
Hand-numbered
Paper wraparound
Screen printing

Published in Berlin, *mono.kultur* is a quarterly arts magazine, each issue of which is dedicated to a single artist or cultural figure. The design of each issue is specially tailored to its subject, often by freelance designers who are invited to 'guest produce' a particular issue.

The idea for a collector's box set was conceived at the birth of the magazine, with the publishers holding back copies of each issue for this very purpose. Indeed, viewed by its creators as 'an archive of conversations and ideas', the magazine is well suited to this format. Following on from mono.archiv #01, mono.archiv #02 contains issues 16 to 30.

—

PUBLISHER *Kai von Rabenau, Germany*
ART DIRECTION & DESIGN *mono.studio*
PRODUCTION *mono.kultur*
DATE *2013*

Silversun Pickups
Neck of the Woods

XXXXXXXXXXXXXXXXXX

Specifications
2 coloured 12" vinyl records
7" vinyl record
Blind embossing
Book cloth
Die cutting
Gatefold vinyl sleeve
Hardback book
Slip case with inner box

The Silversun Pickups are a Los Angeles-based alternative rock band; *Neck of the Woods* is their third studio album. The box-set edition is deliberately restrained, in terms of both materials and design. Central to its overall look and feel is the photographic imagery, from the album cover by fine-art photographer Todd Hido to the interior images by music and fashion photographer Autumn de Wilde.

—

PUBLISHER *Dangerbird Records, USA*
ART DIRECTION & DESIGN
Lawrence Azerrad
PHOTOGRAPHY *Todd Hido, Autumn de Wilde, Sandra Steh, James Frost, Sterling Andrews*
DATE *2012*

Shout Out Louds
Blue Ice (The Ice Record Project)

Specifications
Black foil blocking
Distilled water
DIY ice record
Foam
Glass water bottle
Lift-off-lid box
Silicon mould
Edition of 10

To mark the release of *Optica*, their first album in three years, Swedish indie pop band Shout Out Louds sought a new way to create a sense of mystery and introduce the single 'Blue Ice'. The band sent out 'Ice Record Kits' to ten select fans and bloggers, but in order to be the first to hear the single, the kits' recipients had to make the record themselves. This was achieved by pouring water into a mould and then freezing it.

A watertight silicon mould was crafted to enable the record to be removed and played as quickly as possible – a key consideration in the case of records made of ice. A particular challenge was to perfect the grooves on the record itself. Any air bubbles in the ice would prevent the formation of precise grooves, causing the needle to jump. The band's ad agency experimented with various techniques, and eventually settled on the use of distilled water to reduce the impurities that would result in imperfections in the record.

—

PUBLISHER *Merge Records, Sweden*
CREATIVE DIRECTION *Kalle Widgren (TBWA)*
CREATIVES *Alexander Fredlund, André Persson, Martin Baude*
DESIGN *Christian Styffe*
PLANNER *Lisa Adamsson*
ACCOUNT MANAGER *Ylva Windolf*
ACCOUNT DIRECTOR *Tobias Bergenwall*
DATE *2012*

⬨⬨⬨⬨⬨⬨⬨⬨⬨⬨⬨⬨⬨⬨⬨

Specifications
5 7" vinyl records
Acrylic
Box with diagonal opening
Debossing
Foil blocking
Hand-numbered
Microfibre cleaning cloth
Record spindle
Screen printing
Edition of 500

To celebrate its fifth anniversary, London-based record label Erased Tapes wanted to produce something limited and special for its fans. In the end, the decision was made to create a box set of five 7" records. The box itself is made from heavyweight, high-quality card that has been dyed black, manually debossed and folded. The 7" format was chosen because it neatly divides the ten songs in the box set – one by each of the ten artists signed to the label at the time – into five discs. Linking the different artists is the record spindle in the shape of the Erased Tapes logo. The addition of an anti-static cleaning cloth was inspired by cleaning instructions found on the liner notes of an old Kraftwerk record.
—

PUBLISHER *Erased Tapes, UK/Germany*
ART DIRECTION *Torsten Posselt, Robert Raths, Sofia Ilyas*
DESIGN *Torsten Posselt (Feld)*
ILLUSTRATION *Chris Hernandez, Herr Müller, Torsten Posselt*
PRODUCTION *The Vinyl Factory, Maren Thomsen*
DATE *2013*

Erased Tapes
Collection V

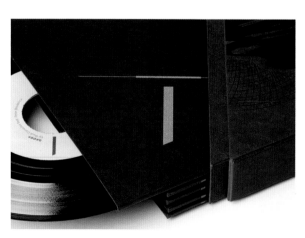

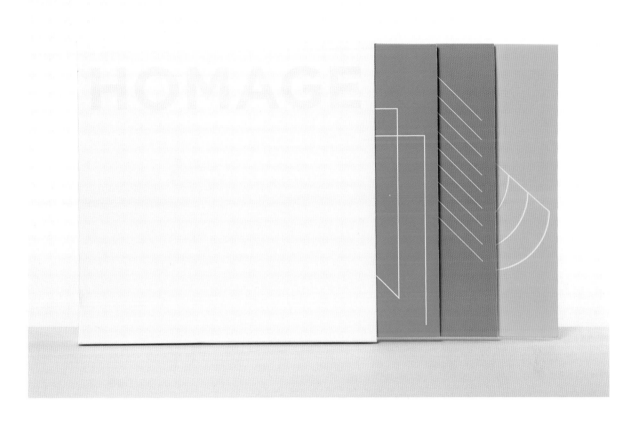

Eleh
Homage

⬦⨯⨯⨯⨯⨯⨯⨯⨯⨯⨯⨯⨯⨯⨯⨯⨯⨯⬦

Specifications
3 12" vinyl records
Hand-numbered
Screen printing
Slip case
Spot gloss UV varnish
Edition of 800

John Brien's striking, soundwave-like artwork for *Homage*, a limited-edition reissue of three previously unavailable albums by Eleh, suggests with great simplicity the restrained, minimalist music produced by this 'electroacoustic' artist. The colour of each album sleeve echoes that of the original release, while all three records are housed in a rigid white slip case on to which the word 'Homage' has been printed using spot varnish.

—
PUBLISHER *Taiga Records, USA*
ART DIRECTION *Eleh*
DESIGN *John Brien*
PRODUCTION *Stoughton Printing Co.,
VGKids, Pirates Press*
DATE *2013*

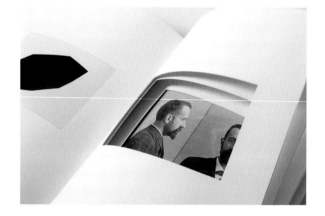

Stéphanie Solinas
Sans titre, M. Bertillon

Specifications
Cut pages
Hand-numbered
Hand-signed
Hardback book
Mounted paper mask
Wood and Plexiglass box
Edition of 23

Sans titre, M. Bertillon is partly based on the theories of Alphonse Bertillon, the French nineteenth-century pioneer of anthropometrics. For the special edition of the book, the Bertillon mask has already been assembled by the book's creator, artist Stéphanie Solinas; with the standard edition, this must be done by the reader, by cutting out the individual parts and sticking them together with glue (an online video by Solinas shows how it is done). To ensure that each special edition is unique, Solinas leaves a different piece uncut from the book every time she assembles a mask, resulting in twenty-three different covers.

—

PUBLISHER *RVB Books, France*
ART DIRECTION *Stéphanie Solinas, Remi Faucheux*
DESIGN *Stéphanie Solinas*
PHOTOGRAPHY *Stéphanie Solinas*
PRODUCTION *Bubu*
DATE *2012*

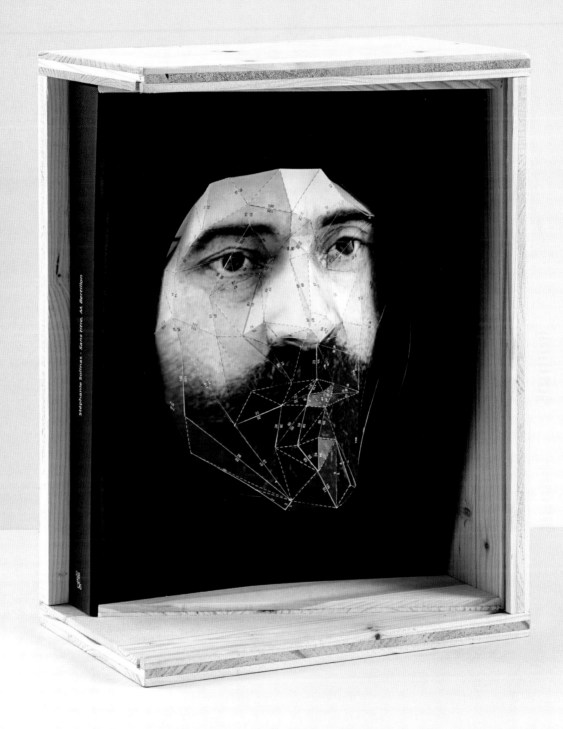

Gustav Mahler
Lied

In 2011 the Gustav Mahler
Festival in Vienna combined
performances of the Austrian
composer's lieder (art songs)
with striking digital imagery.
The results of this experiment
can be found in *Lied*: seven
DVDs of the performances and a
hardback book. Mahler's source of
inspiration for his songs, nature,
also inspired the abstract, black-
and-white floral collages used
throughout the *Lied* box set.

—

PUBLISHER *Departure, Austria*
ART DIRECTION *Eva Dranaz*
DESIGN *3007*
ILLUSTRATION *Eva Dranaz*
PRODUCTION *Rema Print, G+G*
DATE *2011*

◇◇◇◇◇◇◇◇◇◇◇◇◇◇◇◇◇◇◇◇

Specifications
2 different blacks
7 DVDs
Hardback book
Offset printing
Slip case

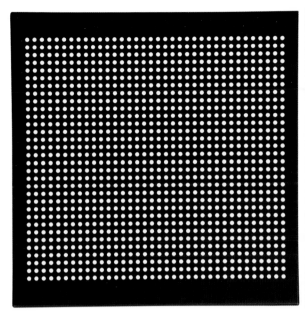

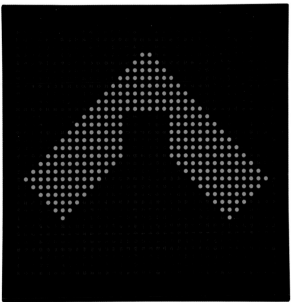

Squarepusher
Ufabulum

Specifications
2 12" vinyl records
Booklet
CD
Glow-in-the-dark ink
Lift-off-lid box
Screen printing

The special vinyl edition of *Ufabulum*, an album by British recording artist Squarepusher (Tom Jenkins), is packaged in a black rigid box. Part of the box's lid has been printed with glow-in-the-dark ink: when the lights go out, the Squarepusher logo is revealed.

—

PUBLISHER *Warp, UK*
ART DIRECTION *Tom Jenkinson,*
Nick Robertson
DESIGN *Nick Robertson*
PHOTOGRAPHY *Donald Milne*
PRODUCTION *James Burton (Warp)*
DATE *2012*

The Horrors
Higher

◇◇◇◇◇◇◇◇◇◇◇◇◇◇◇◇

Specifications
2 CDs
4 12" vinyl records
DVD
Fine-grained linen
Foil blocking
Matt lamination
Silk ribbon
Slip case with inner box
Spot gloss UV varnish

Higher is a deluxe edition of the singles and videos from *Skying*, the third studio album by British alternative rock group The Horrors; also included are cover versions and reworkings of the original songs by a variety of different recording artists. Designer Alison Fielding worked very closely with the band at each stage of the project, which was a year in the making.

Every detail of the design was carefully considered, from the shape of the box to the pattern on the ribbon, and numerous product samples were seen. The intention was to create a luxurious-looking product, with linings, special finishes and back-printing. Fielding decided that the overall design should have a stripped-back feel, and Leif Podhajsky was the third illustrator to be commissioned for the project. Fortunately, Fielding felt that he had 'got it right', producing images that were sympathetic to the existing concept.

—

PUBLISHER *XL Recordings, UK*
ART DIRECTION & DESIGN
Alison Fielding
ILLUSTRATION *Leif Podhajsky*
DATE *2012*

Fiona Tan
Vox Populi, London

◇◇◇◇◇◇◇◇◇◇◇◇◇◇◇◇◇◇

Specifications
5 paperback books
5 photographic prints
Art print
Blind debossing
Card folder
Colorado book cloth
Hand-numbered
Hand-signed
Letterpress printing
Slip case
Edition of 10

Fiona Tan's *Vox Populi* series offers a 'snapshot' of five different locations – Norway, Sydney, Tokyo, Switzerland and London – through photographs taken from family albums. Here, all five books in the series are accompanied by five photographic prints, one for each location, and a numbered and signed 'photographic plan' by the artist showing how the prints should be arranged.

—

PUBLISHER *Book Works, UK*
ART DIRECTION *Fiona Tan*
DESIGN *Gabriele F. Gotz*
PHOTOGRAPHY *Sourced from family albums by Fiona Tan*
PRODUCTION *Lecturis, Book Works Studio*
DATE *2012*

Kishi Bashi
7" Box Set

Specifications
3 'splatter' 7" vinyl records
Hand-numbered
Hand-signed
Semi-gloss
Wooden box
Edition of 500

This limited-edition box set contains three singles taken from American musician Kishi Bashi's debut album, *151a* (2012), each of which is backed by an unreleased orchestral cover version. The triptych-style artwork combines references to the songs' lyrics with the bright colour palette and other design elements used for the album's cover art. The records themselves feature a distinctive two-colour 'splatter' design.

—

PUBLISHER *Joyful Noise Recordings, USA*
DESIGN *David J. Woodruff*
PRODUCTION *Zach Petersen*
(Deep Wood Workshop)
DATE *2013*

Slanted
Issue 21: Cuba – The New Generation

Specifications
17 art prints
CD
Cigar box
Embossing
Etching
Fluorescent inks
Gabon redwood
Letterpress printing
Magazine
Pen and ink
Screen printing
Spot UV varnish
Stamping
Edition of 50

This special edition of the typography and graphic design magazine *Slanted* showcases the work of a new generation of Cuban typographers, designers, photographers and illustrators, with a particular focus on Cuban poster art. The idea of devoting an entire issue to this body of work originated with French graphic designer Natalie Seisser, who has been travelling to Cuba for many years.

The intention behind the design of the special edition was to give the reader a sense of Cuba's visual diversity. Bright colours are mixed with black and white on an unusual paper stock, providing the reader with a sensory feast as they flip through the pages. According to the publishers, the decision to present the magazine in a specially made Cuban cigar box was a natural one. The magazine itself is accompanied by a CD and a set of art prints.

—

PUBLISHER *Magma Brand Design, Germany*
CREATIVE DIRECTION *Lars Harmsen*
(Editor-in-Chief, Slanted)
ART DIRECTION *Falko Gerlinghoff,*
Markus Lange
GRAPHIC DESIGN *Julia Kahl*
PRODUCTION *E&B Engelhardt und Bauer,*
Gruber Druck und Medien, Falko Gerlinghoff,
Markus Lange, Schuster Custom Woodworking
DATE *2013*

Popol Vuh
The Werner Herzog
Soundtracks

Specifications
5 CDs
Black silk ribbon
Hardback book
Matt lamination
Slip case

The music of Popol Vuh, a German avant-garde rock band founded by Florian Fricke, is inextricably linked to the films of Werner Herzog, for which the group composed many of the soundtracks. This box set contains Popol Vuh's scores for five of Herzog's early feature films: *Aguirre, The Wrath of God* (1972), *Heart of Glass* (1976), *Nosferatu* (1978), *Fitzcarraldo* (1982) and *Cobra Verde* (1987). Accompanying the five CDs is a ninety-eight-page hardback book containing liner notes and unseen film stills.

—

PUBLISHER *Edition Popol Vuh and SPV, Germany*
CREATIVE DIRECTION *Johannes Fricke, Chris Rehberger, Gero Herrde (SPV)*
DESIGN *Chris Rehberger, Double Standards*
PHOTOGRAPHY *Bettina von Waldthausen, Werner Herzog Film Production*
DATE *2011*

The Clarke & Ware Experiment
House of Illustrious

◇◇◇◇◇◇◇◇◇◇◇◇◇◇◇◇◇

Specifications
10 CDs
Certificate of authenticity
Clear cast acrylic
Foam block
Hand-numbered
Hand-signed
High-density foam
Laser etching
Polypropylene film
Spindle with circular endplates
Stainless steel
Edition of 1,000

The Clarke & Ware Experiment is a collaboration between British musicians Vince Clarke (Erasure, Depeche Mode, Yazoo) and Martyn Ware (Human League, Heaven 17). The *House of Illustrious* box set, which took almost eighteen months to design, brings together the duo's first two albums and eight CDs of unreleased material.

The driving force behind the design of the box set was a desire for it to be truly unique. Kept in place by two acrylic endplates, the ten CDs are held on a stainless-steel spindle; etched into the spindle are the words 'Made in Sheffield', Ware's home town. The housing is made from foam that has been treated with a fine water jet, giving it a solid, granite-like feel that belies its fragility. The laser-etched type on the foam recalls traditional mason-cut lettering.
—

PUBLISHER *Mute, UK*
ART DIRECTION *Malcolm Garrett (Images&Co)*
DESIGN *Malcolm Garrett, Martyn Ware, Tim Milne (Artomatic)*
PRODUCTION *Artomatic, Mute*
DATE *2012*

I R M A B O O M

INTERVIEW : MATTHEW LEE

PHOTOGRAPH : IVAN JONES

IRMA BOOM is a Dutch graphic designer and a leading figure in the world of book design. Based in Amsterdam, she has taught at Yale University since 1992, and in recent years has worked on commissions from Dutch architect Rem Koolhaas, Amsterdam's Rijksmuseum and American artist Sheila Hicks. Boom's *JamesJenniferGeorgina* (2013; see page 52) is the story of the Butler family told through postcards, conversations and photographs.

How did you become involved in the *JamesJenniferGeorgina* project?
Jennifer Butler saw an article about me in the *New York Times* and sent me a package containing some sample postcards and a letter asking me to collaborate on the project. When I met the Butlers for the first time, it was at the opening of an exhibition of my work in Zurich. I very much appreciated the fact that they had travelled all the way from France to see it. We decided to meet again and talk about the possibilities of creating a book. I went to Paris to meet them again and to hear the full story. At some point I had the idea that James, Jennifer and Georgina should have conversations together. I always work with numbers, especially the number three, and here there are three people: mother, father and daughter. That's how I came up with twenty-one conversations: seven multiplied by three. And the book was a gift for Georgina's twenty-first birthday. It was a moment to look back and reflect on the past.

It's an incredibly personal – and, at times, painful – project. Did you become emotionally involved, and, if so, how did it affect your work?
We had some intense discussions for a while, but I never felt too involved. I tried to remain objective, and my aim was to make the best book for this special 'triangle' of people. In addition to the conversations, I asked each of them to supply individual texts. The book is completely honest and made with no compromises. That's what makes it special.

Why did you create the unique three-fold binding spine?
Because the book is so thick – 1,200 pages – a hardcover book with one spine wouldn't have opened very well, so I started to experiment in order to solve the problem. This is what I enjoy doing: inventing something new. I always make the dummies of my books myself, and I tried many solutions before I came up with a spine divided into three. Now it may seem like an obvious solution, but it was quite something to get there. I am very happy with the result. It is a direct reference to the content, and it became a distinguishing feature of the book.

Why the bright-yellow book and the grey box?
The choice of yellow was pure intuition. I can't explain it, but it had to be yellow from the very beginning. To protect the book I needed a box. The box is made from an acid-free board.

Why the lack of spacing in the book's title?
I see the three people as a whole, not as three separate individuals.

What do you think of special-edition books?

It goes a little bit against my philosophy. I love big print runs. Books are made to spread information and reach a large audience. That's my reason for making books. Special editions happen because the publishing industry is under pressure, so they think up these limited editions, but I don't like it. You don't make books to become collector's items. Publishers make something rare and hope it will become a collector's item, but that doesn't necessarily happen. If it's not good enough, it won't become collectable.

But this book is limited to 999 copies and costs more than €400. Does that trouble you?

If you make books, you make reproductions and you want to spread information and content. Almost a thousand copies is quite a lot! Sometimes a subject demands a smaller quantity and still reaches the right audience. Because this book was published privately, it didn't receive the same amount of publicity as a more mainstream book. The distribution of the book is therefore much slower.

Do you collect books?

I own a few thousand books. I have five floors in my house, and there are bookshelves on every floor.

What qualities do you look for when buying books?

I especially like books from the 1960s, maybe because they're so conceptual. I also have some books from the seventeenth century.

Has there been a golden age for book-making?

I think it was probably when the book became a mass-produced object. I like the idea of the democracy of the book, although if I were to talk about a golden age for design it would be the 1960s. The golden age of actual book-making was probably the sixteenth century and earlier.

When you work with artists, how do you balance your art with their art?

That's always a big discussion. I wanted to become a painter when I went to art school, so I work in a very autonomous way. I need trust and freedom in order to create something, otherwise I simply won't work.

Have you had differences of opinion with artists?

Oh yes. When I made my book on [Dutch graphic designer] Otto Treumann [*Otto Treumann: Graphic Design in the Netherlands*, 1999], he hated it. I told him I could make a book, but it would be my book. If you ask Otto Treumann for a poster, he'll make an Otto Treumann poster. That's what you want! And when people come to me, they want my book. When I receive a commission, I say to people that I'm not a supermarket. You can't ask for more mayonnaise, more ketchup. That's not how I work. Give me space, freedom and trust, and I'll make a book. With my book for Sheila Hicks, for example, the collaboration went extremely well. It's already on its fourth printing, and it is my manifesto for the book. I'm obsessed with size, scale and weight – the edges of books, the smell of books. They are 3D objects. They're not something you put on an e-reader.

Why do you prefer to talk about 'commissions' rather than 'clients'?
It's a very Dutch thing. We have a word, '*opdrachtgever*', a person who commissions you. It's very different to having a client, which implies that I have to do what they say. I think of my work as being commissioned by 'commissioners', rather than by clients: a collaboration on equal terms, characterized by freedom and trust.

Where do you think your anti-authority streak comes from?
Maybe I need to see a psychiatrist! I'm the youngest child in a large family, and so I always got my way. I always got the last cookie in the jar.

What percentage of proposals do you accept?
Less than half. It's pure instinct when to say yes or no. With *JamesJenniferGeorgina*, Jennifer called many times over the course of two years. Eventually I met the Butlers and gave them my conditions – complete freedom, trust and time – and they said yes. I think it's a really special book. In terms of my career, it's one of the highlights.

Your book on Chanel No. 5 [2013] contains no ink at all – all the images and text have been embossed on to the page. Are there still lots of opportunities for innovation and experimentation in book-making?
Oh yes, this is just the beginning! The only problem is that we still need the craftsmanship – the binders, the printers and all these people with specialized skills. It's terrible that printers and binders keep closing down. I need them to help me create my books. For the Chanel book, it was hard at first because we couldn't find anyone who could actually produce it. After lots of searching, however, we finally found companies that could do it.

How has the rise of digital publishing affected the way you work?
The Internet is a big inspiration. When I started working on *SHV Think Book* [1996, published to celebrate the centenary of Dutch trading company SHV Holdings], it was 1991 and the Internet had barely got off the ground. But during the five years of that project, the early Internet influenced us a great deal. When we were asked to make something unusual, we thought about the non-linear structure of the Internet. We wanted to create the sense of being on a journey, like surfing the web, the idea of finding something you weren't looking for. The fatness of the book – 2,136 pages – is very important. We hoped people would find something that they weren't looking for, and that's why the book has no page numbers. If you place the eight bookmarks in the right position, you will find the title of the book.

Has the rise of digital made people more appreciative of beautiful printed objects?
Maybe. If I buy a book it has to be something I couldn't read as a PDF. But I wouldn't call a book an art object. There was a student at Leiden University who did a study of my work and called it 'Book as Art'. I didn't speak to her once while she was writing her study. She says my books are art, which I totally disagree with. Books are objects to be read. The books on display at my exhibition in Paris [2013] I had used extensively. This is an important part of the concept: it's proof that I use my books. They are not art objects.

'The future for book designers is becoming more and more interesting. I think we are in the Renaissance period of making books. I have to think about why something should be a book and not a website. This challenge makes me want to continue designing books.'

You have said that you love the democratic imperative of the book, the spreading of information at a low cost. But the Internet can spread information almost free of charge …
Making books is a very different process from publishing online. The book designer is an editor and director of texts and images. The result of this work is the freezing of time and information, which is a means of reflection. Compare it to a photograph or a painting. An image at a given moment serves as a reference point in time and space. If you print something, it's unchangeable. The Internet, where everything is in flux, where you can change your mind at any time, has helped me define and articulate my work more precisely than ever before. I understand that it's critical to get it right first time. When people refer you to the Internet, you can never be sure that it's correct. I think it's interesting to explore this notion of frozen information and what that means.

Is there unexplored potential for integrating the digital into the physical – for example, USB drives in books?
I think it's a shame to add a DVD or flash drive to a book. It's unnecessary. I'd rather include a URL in the book so that the reader can find it on the Internet. People ask me all the time, 'Shall we put in this or that?' and I never do it. A book is autonomous and strong and doesn't need these devices. It can manage on its own.

What's the future of the book? And what's your future?
The future for book designers is becoming more and more interesting. I think we are in the Renaissance period of making books. I have to think about why something should be a book and not a website. This challenge makes me want to continue designing books. In the 1990s I felt like stopping after spending five years on the SHV project, and I wanted to study law. But I never moved in that direction and here I am, still making books.

How's your work–life balance? Is book-making your life?
It is. All my friends love books. When [Swiss curator and art historian] Hans-Ulrich Obrist invited people to write something for Twitter, my tweet was: 'Books. Can't get enough.' Book-making is becoming more and more interesting. *Irma Boom was photographed at her studio in Amsterdam, The Netherlands*

Jennifer Butler & Irma Boom
JamesJenniferGeorgina

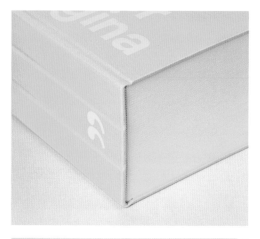

Specifications
Acid-free board
Box
Foil stamping
Hardback book
Linen book cloth
Screen printing
Edition of 999

JamesJenniferGeorgina is the story of the Butler family – husband James, wife Jennifer and daughter Georgina – told using a variety of narrative devices. The first part of the 1,200-page book consists of a selection of the 1,136 postcards sent to Georgina by her parents over the course of ten years of travel. This is followed by transcripts of twenty-one family conversations and a series of family photographs. Key to the book's design is the innovative three-part spine, without which it could not easily be opened. It also neatly reflects both the content and the structure of the book itself.

—

PUBLISHER *Erasmus Publishing Ltd, UK*
CONCEPT & DESIGN *Irma Boom*
PHOTOGRAPHY *Erwin Olaf*
PRINTING *Lenoirschuring*
BINDING *Boekbinderij Van Waarden*
DATE *2010*

For this box set of new and previously released material by Norwegian trumpeter Arve Henriksen, designer Kim Hiorthøy decided to combine new and existing artwork. While the labels of the previously released albums refer back to the artwork of the original records, a new design links the box, the new album, the DVDs and the booklet. Juxtaposed images of foliage were used to suggest change and the passing of time, concepts often associated with the meaning of the title of the new album, *Chron*. To fit with the overall look and feel of the design, the album sleeves were made from inexpensive brown packing paper.
—

PUBLISHER *Rune Grammofon, Norway*
ART DIRECTION & DESIGN *Kim Hiorthøy*
PHOTOGRAPHY *Kim Hiorthøy*
PRODUCTION *Optimal Media*
DATE *2012*

Arve Henriksen
Solidification

◇◇◇◇◇◇◇◇◇◇◇◇◇◇◇◇◇◇◇◇

Specifications
2 DVDs
7 12" vinyl records
Booklet
Lift-off-lid box
Offset printing
Uncoated card

Can
The Lost Tapes

Specifications
3 CDs
Booklet
Lift-off-lid box
Uncoated board
Uncoated paper

During the dismantling of the legendary Can studio in Weilerswist, a town on the outskirts of Cologne in Germany, a set of unidentified master tapes was found and stored in the archive of Spoon Records, the independent record label founded in 1979 to release Can's music. No one was sure what was on these tapes until Irmin Schmidt, a founding member of the experimental rock band, and long-time collaborator Jono Podmore started to sift through the more than thirty hours of music.

The Lost Tapes is a selection of what they discovered – not out-takes, but live recordings, rehearsal tapes, studio jams, soundtracks to unreleased films and tracks that failed to make it on to the final versions of albums owing to a lack of space. Fittingly, the box containing the CDs and booklet has been designed to resemble one of the boxes in which the lost tapes were found.
—

PUBLISHER *Spoon Records/Mute, UK*
ART DIRECTION & DESIGN
Julian House (Intro)
PRODUCTION *Mute*
DATE *2012*

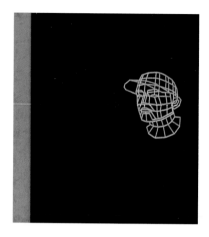

Specifications

7 CDs
12" vinyl record
Black acrylic
Black foil blocking
Booklet
Certificate of authenticity
Debossing
Die cutting
DVD
Embossing
Engraving
Gloss lamination
Glow-in-the-dark ink
Hand-numbered
Hand-signed
Hardback book
Recycled card
Slip case
Uncoated board
Wire binding
Edition of 500

DJ Shadow
Reconstructed

When asked by Island Records to help design the special edition of *Reconstructed*, a retrospective of the work of DJ Shadow (Josh Davis), London-based art director, designer and producer Trevor Jackson thought that it made perfect sense, having worked with the American DJ on several musical collaborations. The label's original idea for the box set was modified by both DJ Shadow and Jackson, who wanted to create something far more desirable, limited and exciting.

Inside the slip case is a white hardback book, the two 'pages' of which contain the booklet and the 12" record; the seven CDs and single DVD are housed in the book's inside front and back covers. The engraved graphic on the front of the slip case has been infilled with glow-in-the-dark ink – because, says Jackson, 'shadows can't exist without light'.

The project took almost twelve months to complete, from initial concept to finished product, with Jackson pushing every production process as far as it would go. 'Along the way,' he says, 'there were numerous manufacturing problems, but most of them actually led to both visual and structural improvements.'

—

PUBLISHER *Island Records/Universal Music Group, USA*
ART DIRECTION & DESIGN *Trevor Jackson*
PRODUCTION *Daniel Mason (Something Else)*
DATE *2012*

Mumford & Sons
The Road to Red Rocks

Specifications

180gsm 12" 'virgin' vinyl record
Art print
Book cloth
CD
DVD
Gold foil blocking
Hardback book
Lift-off-lid box
Overwrapped rigid board
Screen printing

At the heart of this Grammy Award-nominated box set is a hardback book documenting Mumford & Sons' travels during the summer of 2012. Focusing on the British band's self-curated 'Stopovers' – a series of one-day mini-festivals – it follows the band from the UK to the United States, where they ended their tour with a two-night stint at the iconic Red Rocks Amphitheatre in Colorado.

Together with a live DVD and the 'deluxe' CD version of the band's second album, *Babel*, the box set comes with a recording of the Red Rocks performances on heavyweight vinyl. Informing the design of the whole box set was a sense that music should be presented in a physical form and experienced in its entirety. The aim was to offer fans an alternative to the way in which most music is now consumed: downloaded or streamed track by track, at the listener's will.

—

PUBLISHER *Gentlemen of the Road/Island Records, UK*
ART DIRECTION & DESIGN *Ross Stirling (Studio Juice)*
PHOTOGRAPHY *Ted Dwane, Marcus Haney*
PRODUCTION *Modo*
DATE *2012*

Specifications

12 12" vinyl records
Bookmark with download code
Die cutting
Embossing
Hand-numbered
Orange linen
Paperback book
Poster
Slip case with inner box
Edition of 365

Julian Sartorius
Beat Diary

Referring to 2011, the Swiss drummer and 'sound forager' Julian Sartorius made the following pledge: 'Every day I will record one beat, no matter where I am, using the situation each day will bring. Rules: no loops, no effects. Just me, my surroundings, my drum kit and a field recorder allowing overdubs.' The results – more than half of which were released on a daily basis on Sartorius's blog between January and mid-July that year – can be heard in their entirety on *Beat Diary*.

Consisting of twelve LPs, a book containing 365 photos and a poster, *Beat Diary* tells the story of Sartorius's year of rhythm, taking in kitchens, Berlin, mountains, hotel rooms and backstage areas along the way. The beats themselves include the snap of a light switch, the hum of a vacuum cleaner, the squeak of a plastic pig, the rattle of a piano, the buzz of an electric toothbrush, the turn of a music box and, finally, the bang of a firework on New Year's Eve.

—

PUBLISHER *Everestrecords/Kommode Verlag, Switzerland*
ART DIRECTION *Michael Meienberg, Matthias Hügli, Julian Sartorius, Anneka Beatty*
DESIGN *Anneka Beatty*
PHOTOGRAPHY *Julian Sartorius*
PRINTING *Hornberger Druck GmbH*
DATE *2012*

Oasis
Dig Out Your Soul

◇◇◇◇◇◇◇◇◇◇◇◇◇◇◇◇

Specifications
2 CDs
4 12" vinyl records
Black foam studs
Black lined board
Clear gloss foil stamping
Debossing
DVD
Hardback book
Matt lamination
Shoulder box
Spot gloss UV varnish

The artwork for the special edition of *Dig Out Your Soul*, the seventh and final studio album by Oasis, was inspired by English Pop art, English surrealism, Lewis Carroll and the underground press of the 1960s. The intention was to evoke the super-saturated 'now' aesthetic of a lot of late 1960s imagery; the use of collage on most surfaces of the box set, as well as throughout the book, was therefore a natural choice. In the case of the vinyl sleeves, an accumulative effect was created by adding more and more elements to the same collaged image. The designers also wanted the box set to have the feel of an old first edition, hence the use of book cloth for the box and marbled endpapers for the book.
—

PUBLISHER *Big Brother Recordings Ltd, UK*
ART DIRECTION & DESIGN
Julian House (Intro)
ILLUSTRATION *Julian House*
PRODUCTION *Modo*
DATE *2008*

Autechre
Exai

Specifications
4 12" vinyl records
Clear foil blocking
Rigid board
Slip case

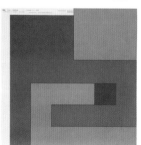

According to the project's designer, the overall look and feel of the special edition of *Exai* – the eleventh album by British electronic music duo Autechre – had two principal sources: conversations with the duo themselves (Rob Brown and Sean Booth) about the thinking behind the album, and the work the designer had created for the previous Autechre release, *Oversteps* (2010). While the design of *Oversteps* was about 'human aspiration to emulate the perfection of the machines we build' (represented by a circular motif), *Exai*, graphically,

'represents our failure to do so'. It is, he continues, about 'the fading ripples of dead technologies and the slow disintegration of designed form'.

Each of the four records included in the box set comes in its own printed inner sleeve. The box itself is covered in Cairn Eco Kraft paper, which has been foil-blocked with a design that echoes the artwork used on the individual record sleeves.

—

PUBLISHER *Warp, UK*
ART DIRECTION & DESIGN *Ian Anderson (The Designers Republic)*
PRODUCTION *Lionel Skerratt (Warp)*
DATE *2013*

❖❖❖❖❖❖❖❖❖❖❖❖❖❖❖

Specifications
4 spot colours
5 7" vinyl records
Gloss varnish
Lift-off-lid box
Velvet lamination

My Wet Calvin are an alternative rock duo from Greece, renowned as much for their stage antics as for their music. *Happened Before* was recorded with five different music producers, who each oversaw the recording of two different tracks – hence the five-record format. Each record carries a different colour: the three primary colours plus black and white. This palette is carried over into a strict grid pattern on the outside of the box. While the overall concept brings to mind the CMYK printing process, the box set, which was designed by the duo themselves, was printed using four Pantone colours.

—

PUBLISHER *Inner Ear Records, Greece*
ART DIRECTION *Aris Nikolopoulos*
DESIGN *Leonidas Ikonomou*
DATE *2012*

My Wet Calvin
Happened Before

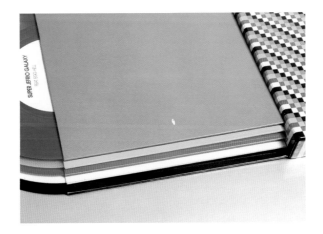

Amon Tobin
Amon Tobin

〰〰〰〰〰〰〰〰〰〰〰〰〰

Specifications
2 DVDs
4 limited-edition cards
6 10" vinyl records
7 CDs
Black MDF
Bolts
Die cutting
Duplex card
Grey board
Lamination
Letterpress printing
Matt-grey foil blocking
Poster
Screen printing
Wing nuts
Edition of 4,000

For the *Amon Tobin* box set, the creative team at Oscar & Ewan design studio took their inspiration from the Brazilian's music, an eclectic mix of the organic and the industrial. This in turn led them to the idea of a vintage flower press. 'We also felt', explain the designers, 'that the action of collecting flowers and saving them not only resonated with much of Amon's way of sampling, but also worked with the fact that this was a limited-edition release. We wanted to bring in that collector element.' In order to heighten the industrial feel, the designers worked closely with London-based Think Tank Media to produce a mix of rough and dark materials, which are held together with a set of bolts fastened with wing nuts. The whole production process was captured in a 'making of' video by Kayalight Studios.

—
PUBLISHER *Ninja Tune, UK*
ART DIRECTION & DESIGN *Oscar & Ewan*
PHOTOGRAPHY *Oscar & Ewan*
PRODUCTION *Think Tank Media*
DATE *2012*

The Breeders
LSXX

In 2013 British independent record label 4AD decided to mark the twentieth anniversary of one of its most famous releases, The Breeders' *Last Splash*, by producing the ultimate version of the album. Curated by the band's members, *LSXX* brings together a selection of existing recordings, unreleased material and unpublished photographs. The task of re-imagining the look of an iconic album created twenty years earlier fell to British graphic designer Vaughan Oliver, the long-time 4AD collaborator who had created the original artwork.

—

PUBLISHER *4AD, UK*
ART DIRECTION *Vaughan Oliver (v23)*
DESIGN *Vaughan Oliver, Philip Laslett, Shesley Crustna, Chris Glass*
PHOTOGRAPHY *Jason Love, Kevin Westenberg, Davy Evans*
PRODUCTION *Greg Muir*
DATE *2013*

Specifications
3 12" vinyl records
4 10" vinyl records
Beize-finished foam
Booklet
Die cutting
Dye
Embossing
Green beize
Laser cutting
Lift-off-lid box
Spot gloss UV varnish
Spot metallic silver

Air
Le Voyage dans la lune

Specifications
4 12" vinyl records
Art print
Debossing
Gold foil blocking
Hand-numbered
Hand-signed
Lift-off-lid box
Edition of 300

In 1993 a long-lost hand-painted colour print – the only one known to exist – of Georges Méliès's classic silent film *Le Voyage dans la lune* (1902) was rediscovered in Spain. It was in very poor condition, however, and so in 1999 two French film foundations, Fondation Groupama Gan and Fondation Technicolor, began the highly delicate work of restoring and digitizing the film.

Eager to put a contemporary spin on Méliès's work and help it reach a new audience, the foundations approached French music duo Air and asked them to compose an original soundtrack. Following the film's debut at the Cannes Film Festival on 11 May 2011, Air decided to develop the soundtrack into an album inspired by the film. The artwork for this limited-edition version reflects the era in which the film was made, using stills from the film itself together with typography typical of the period.

—

PUBLISHER *The Vinyl Factory, UK*
ART DIRECTION & DESIGN *Laurent Pinon in collaboration with Air*
PHOTOGRAPHY *Georges Méliès*
ILLUSTRATION *Georges Méliès*
PRODUCTION *The Vinyl Factory*
DATE *2012*

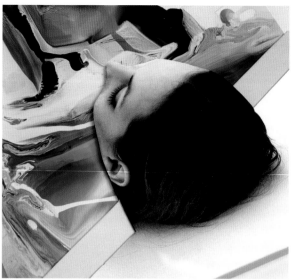

The National
Trouble Will Find Me

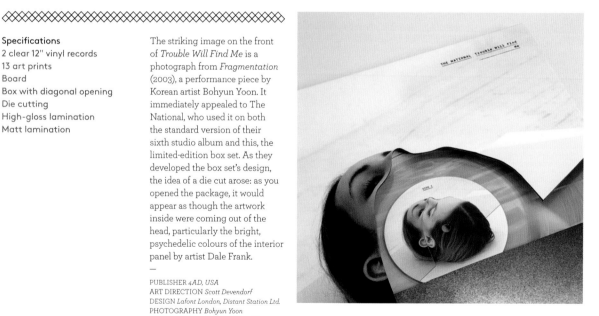

Specifications
2 clear 12" vinyl records
13 art prints
Board
Box with diagonal opening
Die cutting
High-gloss lamination
Matt lamination

The striking image on the front of *Trouble Will Find Me* is a photograph from *Fragmentation* (2003), a performance piece by Korean artist Bohyun Yoon. It immediately appealed to The National, who used it on both the standard version of their sixth studio album and this, the limited-edition box set. As they developed the box set's design, the idea of a die cut arose: as you opened the package, it would appear as though the artwork inside were coming out of the head, particularly the bright, psychedelic colours of the interior panel by artist Dale Frank.

—

PUBLISHER *4AD, USA*
ART DIRECTION *Scott Devendorf*
DESIGN *Lafont London, Distant Station Ltd.*
PHOTOGRAPHY *Bohyun Yoon*
ARTWORKS *Doug Bennett, Clara Claus, John Solimine, Nancy Berninger, Charles Wilkin, Karl Jensen, Jessie Henson, Jeff Salem, Jeff Tyson, Randall J. Lane, Jessica Dessner, Megan Craig, Justin David Andersen*
PRODUCTION *A to Z Media*
DATE *2013*

Edgar Martins
The Time Machine

XXXXXXXXXXXXXXXXXXXXXXXXXXXXX

Specifications
Blind debossing
Faux leather
Foil stamping
Hardback book
Solander box
Edition of 300

In 2010 photographer Edgar Martins was granted exclusive access to more than twenty hydroelectric power stations in his native Portugal. Many were built between the 1950s and 1970s, at a time when Portugal was experiencing rapid economic growth and social change. In some cases, they were intended to house up to 250 workers; now, however, as Martins's photographs in *The Time Machine* show, a large number of them are mostly uninhabited, run almost entirely by computers.

According to Martins, the design of *The Time Machine* was inspired by a variety of visual material, including specialized engineering manuals and applied chemistry almanacs. The graphic elements were taken from machine graphs and other technical documentation found on site. The graph on the cover of the clamshell box, for example, was used to chart the flow of water over a given period of time.

—

PUBLISHER *The Moth House, UK*
ART DIRECTION *Edgar Martins, Andre Montenegro*
DESIGN *Andrew Sloat, Kerry Rakowski*
PHOTOGRAPHY *Edgar Martins*
ILLUSTRATION *Andrew Sloat*
PRODUCTION *EBS Verona, The Moth House*
DATE *2011*

⬡⬡⬡⬡⬡⬡⬡⬡⬡⬡⬡⬡⬡⬡⬡⬡⬡⬡⬡⬡⬡⬡⬡

Specifications
Archive box
Cotton wool
Glass test tube
Hand-rubbed artwork
Hawthorn berries
Lamination
Steel nut and bolt
Translucent 7" vinyl record
Translucent 10" vinyl record
Translucent 12" vinyl record
White envelope
White felt washers
White polystyrene foam

According to :zoviet*france:, a
British electronic music collective,
the recordings that make up
7.10.12 were originally intended
to be released as a trilogy of
12" singles, one every few months.
A chance encounter with the year
1691, which is the same when
rotated 180 degrees, led to a wider
consideration of the numerical
properties of certain dates. It soon
became clear to the group that
7 October 2012, when expressed
as 7.10.12, gives the three diameter
sizes (in inches) in which vinyl
records are manufactured. The
project was quickly changed to
a box set containing a 7", a 10"
and a 12" record, to be released
on the seventh day of the tenth
month of the twelfth year. The
hawthorn berries in the glass vial
were taken from the location in
Northumberland where the hand-
rubbings were made.

—

PUBLISHER *Alt Vinyl, UK*
ART DIRECTION & DESIGN *:zoviet*france:*
PRODUCTION *Bang-On, Paragon Cutting
Formes Ltd*
DATE *2012*

:zoviet*france:
7.10.12

Warp
Warp20

XXXXXXXXXXXXXXXXX

Specifications
5 10" vinyl records
5 CDs
Debossing
Embossing
Foil blocking
Gloss lamination
Graining
Hardback folder
Laser etching
Perfect-bound book
Poster
Slip case
Tipped-on artwork
Uncoated board

Released to celebrate the twentieth anniversary of British independent music label Warp, *Warp20* is a special-edition box set containing a mix of new and previously unreleased recordings, as well as some of the label's most popular tracks. Also included is a 192-page book featuring the artwork from every Warp record released between 1989 and August 2009. The photography used throughout the box set is by British photographer Dan Holdsworth, while two of the 10" records were produced using laser etching.
—

PUBLISHER *Warp, UK*
ART DIRECTION & DESIGN *Yes*
PHOTOGRAPHY *Dan Holdsworth*
PRODUCTION *James Burton &*
Lionel Skerratt (Warp), Daniel Mason
(Something Else)
DATE *2009*

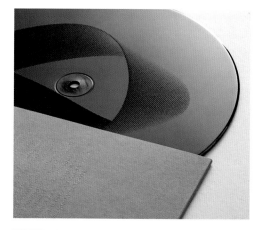

Warp20 (Recreated) Warp20 (Chosen) Warp20 (Elemental)

Warp20 (1989–2009)
The Complete Catalogue
WAP1–WAP280
WARP1–WARP185
20

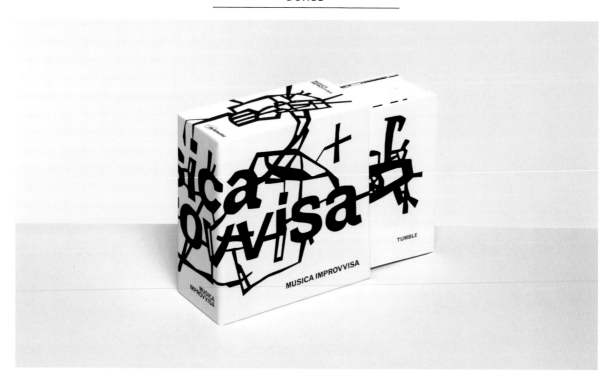

Die Schachtel
Musica Improvvisa

Specifications
1-colour offset printing
10 CDs
Booklet
DVD
Gloss UV varnish
Matt varnish
Poster
Slip case
Edition of 600

The intention behind the design of *Musica Improvvisa*, a collection of recordings by ten avant-garde groups from Italy, was to create a unique visual language capable of reflecting the radical nature of the music. The artwork consists of sketches made in an 'improvisational' style: drawn in unusual contexts, the sketches were later reworked to produce the final designs; the hand-drawn typography was produced in a similar fashion. A stark, black-and-white palette was used throughout to suggest the pared-down nature of the whole project.

—

PUBLISHER *Die Schachtel, Italy*
ART DIRECTION & DESIGN
Bruno Stucchi (Dinamomilano)
ILLUSTRATION *Bruno Stucchi,*
Riccardo Stucchi
PRODUCTION *La Grafica Cremonese*
DATE *2010*

Russian Criminal Tattoo
Encyclopaedia

Specifications
3 hardback books
Gold foil blocking
Hand-numbered
Hand-signed
Photographic print
Solander box
Spiderweb-patterned glassine
Edition of 25 + 5 APs

While working as a guard in St Petersburg's infamous Kresty Prison, Danzig Baldaev recorded more than 3,000 of the inmates' tattoos and their coded meanings. Originally published in three separate volumes, Baldaev's drawings and notes reveal a hitherto unknown world. This limited-edition box set consists of first editions of each volume and a photographic print signed by Sergei Vasiliev, the photographer who took the images used in all three books.

These objects are housed in a solander box. The print is also wrapped in a sheet of spiderweb-patterned glassine, a thin type of paper used in bookbinding. In the world of Russian criminal tattoos, a spider on a web carries several meanings, especially when found on the shoulder. If the spider is facing upwards, then it means that the bearer wants to further his position in the criminal realm; if it is facing downwards, then the bearer longs to leave his life of crime.

—

PUBLISHER *FUEL Publishing, UK*
ART DIRECTION & DESIGN
Damon Murray, Stephen Sorrell (FUEL)
PHOTOGRAPHY *Sergei Vasiliev*
ILLUSTRATION *Danzig Baldaev*
DATE *2008*

WassinkLundgren
Lu Xiaoben

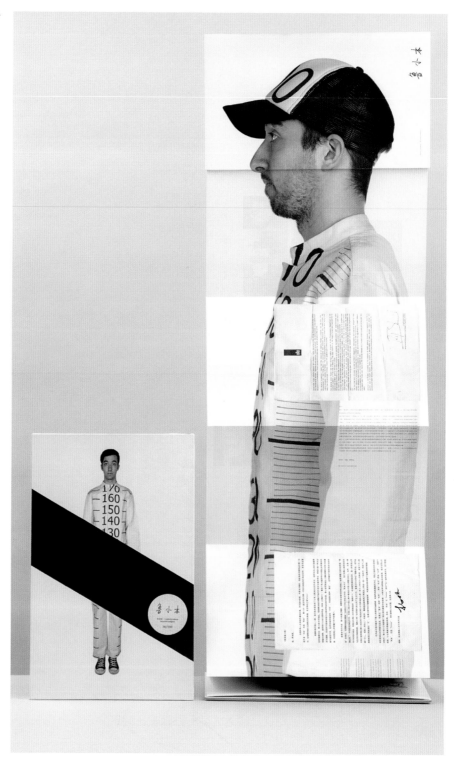

Specifications
Belly band
Cardboard box
DVD
Hand-numbered
Hand-signed
Hardcover leporello
Photographic print
Sticker
Edition of 100

In 2007 Ruben Lundgren – of artist duo WassinkLundgren – moved to Beijing to study for an MA. At 2 metres (6½ feet) tall, Lundgren soon found himself the centre of attention. *Lu Xiaoben,* which translates as 'Little Ben Lu', a reference to London's Big Ben and Lundgren's own status as a tourist attraction, is a record of the Chinese fascination with his height. When fully extended, the leporello, or concertina-fold book, reveals a life-size image of Lundgren in his 'human ruler' suit. This special edition includes a DVD of the artist in Beijing.
—

PUBLISHER *Badger & Press, China*
ART DIRECTION *WassinkLundgren*
DESIGN *Liu Zhizhi*
DATE *2011*

Muse
2nd Law

Specifications
2 12" vinyl records
3 art prints
CD
DVD
Flood coating
Gloss lamination
Lift-off-lid box
Liquid-crystal ink
Rigid board

For the box set of *2nd Law*, the sixth studio album by British rock band Muse, the group wanted to use heat-sensitive packaging to reflect the album's title, a reference to the second law of thermodynamics. The designers' novel solution was to coat the box in thermochromic liquid-crystal ink. The artwork for the record sleeves was created by the Human Connectome Project, which uses neuroimaging to reveal the neural pathways of the human brain.

—

PUBLISHER *Warner Bros. Records, Helium 3, Warner/Chappell, USA*
ART DIRECTION *Muse*
DESIGN *Gareth White, Darren Richards*
NEUROIMAGE *Human Connectome Project*
ILLUSTRATION *Steve Wilson*
PHOTOGRAPHY *Gavin Bond*
PRODUCTION *Modo*
DATE *2012*

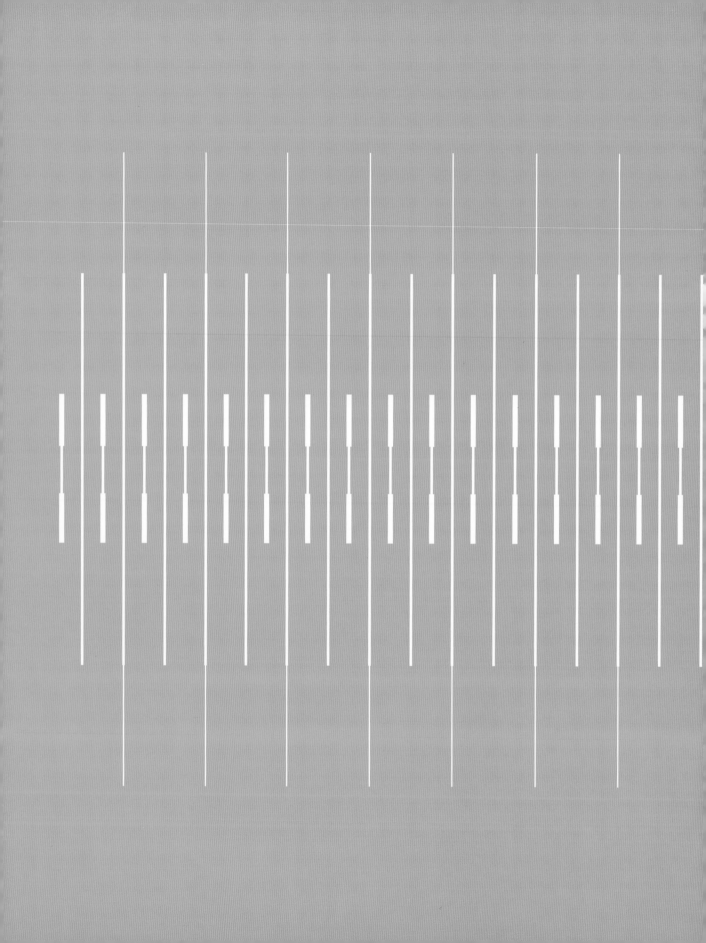

MULTIPLES

Multiple covers, guest artists, collectible series and deluxe editions made from specialist materials

Alec Soth & Lester B. Morrison
Harper's Bazaar
Richard Mosse
David Bowie
The-Dream
Toby Ziegler
Penguin
B°Tong & EMERGE
Yeasayer
Junip
Gabby Young & Other Animals
Glasvegas
The Hunger
Lubomyr Melnyk
Apparat
Atoms for Peace
Bleep
Peter Broderick
Four Corners
Annual
Modeselektor
Cat Power
Pepe Deluxé

Flying Lotus
Woody & Paul
Unoiki
Novum
Penguin
Wilco
Woodkid
Jacqueline Hassink
The Sochi Project
Colors
Coldplay
Lukas Wassmann
Bleep
Marc Romboy & Ken Ishii
Nieves
Bruce Gilden
Wallpaper*
Quentin Blake
Moldover
Reel Art Press
John Carpenter
Penguin

A C

S

O

T

H

INTERVIEW : MATTHEW LEE

PHOTOGRAPH : DANIEL SHEA

ALEC SOTH is a photographer from Minnesota best known for his large-scale, cinematic images of contemporary America. From his Minneapolis studio, Soth also runs a publishing company, Little Brown Mushroom, which specializes in photo books with an emphasis on storytelling. The special edition of *Broken Manual* (2010; see page 84) came packaged in its own hand-glued and hand-cut book-safe, with 300 unique covers.

How did you approach the special edition of *Broken Manual*?
Broken Manual is an incredibly physical book, but it's also a storytelling book, so I tried to piece those two things together. It's about a guy preparing a manual for people who want to run away from their lives. I bought a lot of 'how to change your identity' books online, so I'm probably on some watch list now! At one point in my research, I came across an image of a book-safe. I was intrigued by the idea, so I bought some and photographed them. If you want to run away from your family and you've bought a book on how to do it, what are you going to do with that book? You hide it in a book-safe.

Are you a collector of special editions?
I've done a lot of special editions and I understand the economics – it's a way for publishers to recoup some of their costs – but unfortunately they're very often made as an afterthought. As a collector of photography books, I'm not very interested in the special editions. I just want the regular book. As it happens, the non-special edition of *Broken Manual* was never properly published, so almost half the copies made are special editions. It's a really rare book, which suits the work. The book is about disappearing, and the book barely exists.

Why did you decide to start your own publishing company?
I used to call it my hobby, but it's become much bigger than that. It's a major part of my creative life now. I started it on a whim in 2008 because it was the end of George W. Bush's second term as US president and I wanted to mark that moment. I made a non-narrative publication, a collection of pictures spanning his presidency called *The Last Days of W* [2008], and printed it on newsprint. I made 1,000 copies and made it as cheaply as possible. I found the process thrilling. I became increasingly interested in storytelling, and that's how Little Brown Mushroom came together. Every book combines text and images to tell stories.

Is it this love of storytelling that leads to your preference for books over gallery exhibitions?
Absolutely. The book is a narrative medium with a fixed sequence, whereas exhibitions are ever-changing and give more weight to the individual image.

Has the Internet changed the way photographers present their work in terms of sequencing and storytelling?
For photographers, a phenomenon of the individual image – the 'greatest hit' – has long existed. I always think back to [American photographer] Dennis Stock, who took that famous shot of James Dean in Times Square in 1955. He once pulled me aside at a Magnum event and said to me, 'We're in the business of making iconic images – that's what we do.' But that's not what I want to do. I want to make great books. Sure, my income, my livelihood, may come from those single images, but they're not what motivates me. Personally, I don't struggle with the effect the Internet has had. In 2011 I did this group project with Magnum ['Postcards from America'] where five of us went on the road and posted everything on Tumblr, and it was fascinating to see how we all got caught up in those little pink hearts [which indicate when a user 'likes' a photograph]. I'm intrigued as to why one photo will get 200 hearts and another will get two. But it's the same with a book: one or two images in a book will take on a life of their own, and that's intriguing. But it's not troubling. My eyes are on the book, the bigger prize.

'What I see falling away in all of this are those half-assed print-on-demand books – they're in a no-man's-land. They're not a special object, and in terms of the format and distribution, the economics don't work.'

What's been the impact of high-quality cameras on mobile phones? Everybody can take photographs anywhere and publish them instantly ...
It's caused this information glut, with millions of images being produced. In a world of millions of images, millions of fragments, I'm interested in storytelling as a solution. I want to find meaning by stringing some of these fragments together in some kind of narrative.

Are e-books beginning to have an impact on photography publishing?
I think what's happening in publishing is analogous to what happened in music. In most cases you'll have the equivalent of the download, which is the most efficient and cheapest way of distributing photography. But there will continue to be a market for the equivalent of vinyl: well-printed, well-crafted books that have the mark of the author. It makes sense that the vast majority of photographic work will be viewed online, but with a great photography book there's the physicality, the storytelling, the feel of the cover, the sense of its age ...

Do publishers need to be more creative in their approach to book design?
Yes, and they have been. What I see falling away in all of this are those half-assed print-on-demand books – they're in a no-man's-land. They're not a special object, and in terms of the format and distribution, the economics don't work. I get sent a lot of these and they all look the same. They're really off-putting.

You own a vast library of photography books. What draws you to collecting?
The other day my wife was reminiscing about how years ago I had one shelf of books and I was so proud of it. At the time it was a big collection. I live in Minnesota, where I can't see a new exhibition every week and I can't just go to a library and get what I need. So I feel as though my collection is primarily a resource for my work. If I suddenly get an interest in something, then I can turn to it. I'm not interested in signed first editions or any of that stuff. The primary impulse behind my collecting is research.
Alec Soth was photographed in Long Island City, Queens, New York, USA

Alec Soth & Lester B. Morrison
Broken Manual

||||||||||||||||||||||||||||

Specifications
Art print
Booklet
Hand cutting
Hand gluing
Hand-numbered
Hand-signed
Paperback book
Photographic print
Unique book-safe
Edition of 300

Created over a four-year period, photographer Alec Soth's book *Broken Manual* investigates the places to which people retreat when they want to escape civilization. This is not, however, a conventional record of life 'off the grid'. Instead, working with the writer Lester B. Morrison, Soth has created an underground instruction manual for those who wish to escape their lives.

Somewhat unusually, this special edition of *Broken Manual* was published before the standard edition. Limited to 300 copies, each with a unique cover, this is what Soth calls the 'ideal edition' of *Broken Manual*. Every copy of the book is housed inside a one-of-a-kind book-safe. These 'shell' books, which have been cut by hand, also contain a booklet and a signed and numbered photographic print.
—

PUBLISHER *Steidl, Germany/LBM, USA*
PHOTOGRAPHY *Alec Soth*
DATE *2010*

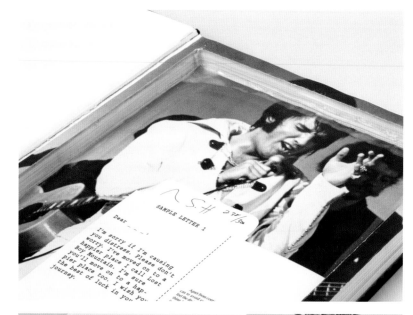

Specifications
Magazine
Edition of 200

In 2013 *Harper's Bazaar* asked British artist Tracey Emin to write an article about David Bowie for the April 2013 issue of the magazine. The article would in many ways be a response to a piece written by Bowie about Emin a few years earlier for the magazine *Modern Painters*. It was also intended to tie in with the release of *The Next Day*, Bowie's first album in a decade, and the major exhibition about the musician that was due to open at London's Victoria and Albert Museum in late March that year.

This limited-edition cover was created by Emin to accompany the article. Based on an already existing artwork by Emin, *You Loved Me Like a Distant Star* (2012), which she felt nicely reflected her feelings for Bowie, it includes the handwritten message 'Thank You Mr Bowie. Tracey Emin, 2013', which was scanned and superimposed on to the artwork. The 200 copies of the magazine featuring Emin's cover were sold exclusively at the V&A.

—

PUBLISHER *Hearst Magazines UK*
ART DIRECTION *Marissa Bourke*
COVER ART *Tracey Emin*
DATE *2013*

Harper's Bazaar
You Loved Me Like a Distant Star

At the heart of *Infra*, Irish photographer Richard Mosse's first book, is the question of how to depict a conflict as complex and intractable as the ongoing war in the Democratic Republic of the Congo. For his photographs of the country and its people, Mosse has used a type of infrared film that renders the green landscape in vivid hues of lavender, crimson and hot pink, thereby throwing his subjects into sharp relief.

The book's clothbound cover features a screen-printed design inspired by the Congolese flag, with pink for the stripe instead of red. At the back of the book are a number of essays printed in pink and red ink, a combination meant to evoke not only the colours of the photographs but also the blood that has been shed by the many years of fighting.

—

PUBLISHER *Aperture Foundation, USA*
DESIGN *Emily Lessard*
PHOTOGRAPHY *Richard Mosse*
PRODUCTION *Trifolio*
DATE *2012*

Specifications
Book cloth
Hardback book
Edition of 500

Richard Mosse
Infra

David Bowie
David Bowie Is

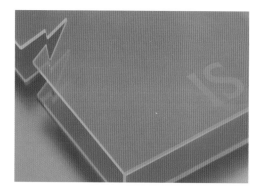

||||||||||||||||||||||||||||||||

Specifications
Coloured ribbons
Embossing
Hand-numbered
Hand-signed
Hardback book
Laser cutting
Metallic ink
Mirror-foiled paper edges
Neon-orange acrylic
Slip case
Tipped-in lithograph
White book cloth
Edition of 500

Published to accompany the David Bowie exhibition held at the Victoria and Albert Museum in 2013, *David Bowie Is* showcases a rich variety of visual material from Bowie's career, including costumes, portraits, lyric sheets and drawings. To anchor this material, the designer used a bright orange accent – a colour that reappears throughout Bowie's aesthetic.

For the standard edition, the bright orange was applied to the cover image, rooting it in the language of the exhibition. For the special edition of 500 copies, the designer used orange on the acrylic slip case. The book itself is bound in white cloth, but becomes orange when inside the case. This particular acrylic was chosen because in low light it emits a refractive glow, giving the box a playful physicality.

The cover of the special edition is printed with a metallic silver, a colour chosen to suggest platinum discs; this same colour appears on the edges of the book block. Blind embossing was used for the colophon, and Bowie's signature appears on a print bound into the first four pages. The intention was to create a desirable object that would not only capture the spirit of the exhibition but also survive as a significant record of Bowie's extraordinary career.
—

PUBLISHER *V&A Publishing, UK*
ART DIRECTION & DESIGN
Jon Abbott, Jonathan Barnbrook
PHOTOGRAPHY *Richard Davis,*
Eileen Travell
DATE *2013*

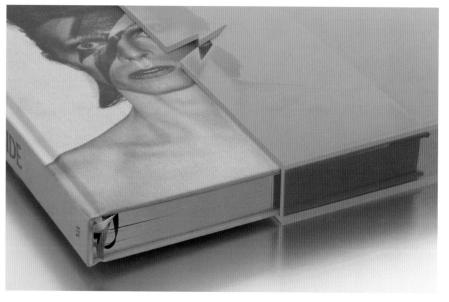

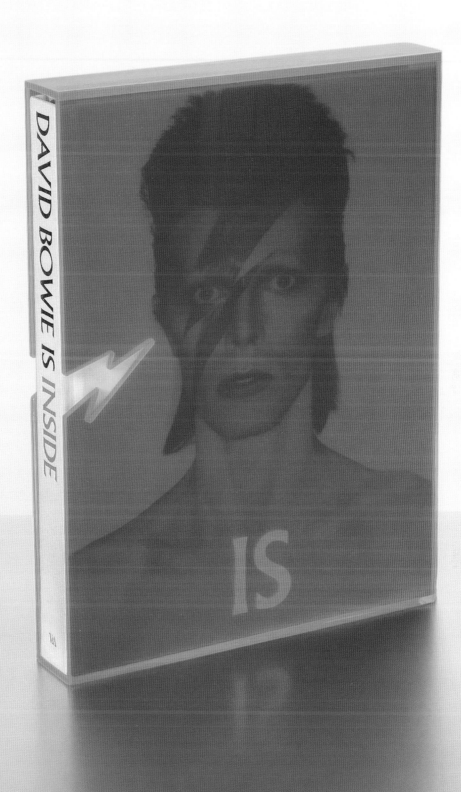

The-Dream
IV Play

||||||||||||||||||||||||||||||||

Specifications
6-panel CD wallet
Booklet
CD
Pyramid fold
Spot gloss UV varnish
Spot matt UV varnish

The artwork for *IV Play*, the fifth studio album by American R&B singer-songwriter and producer The-Dream (aka Terius Nash), is a visual representation of the various aspects of love: pleasure, pain, romance, sex, doubt, rejection, desire. Each of these qualities and emotions is depicted on one of the six panels that make up the CD softpack.

The-Dream's intention was for the album to have a physical component equally as compelling as the music. The central panels of the CD wallet can be folded together to form a pyramid, while the booklet features triangular-shaped liner notes. Gloss and matt spot varnishes lend texture to the whole package.

—

PUBLISHER *Island Def Jam Music Group, USA*
CREATIVE DIRECTION *Todd Russell, Terius 'The-Dream' Nash*
ART DIRECTION *Todd Russell, Kristen Yiengst*
DESIGN *Todd Russell*
ILLUSTRATION *Joe Zeff Design*
PHOTOGRAPHY *Andrew Zaeh*
DATE *2013*

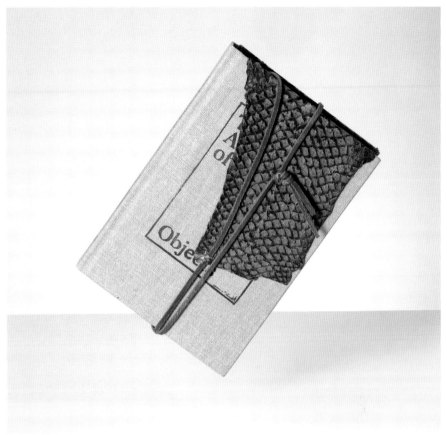

||||||||||||||||||||||||||||||||

Specifications
Animal skins (ray, carp)
Foil stamping
Hand-signed
Hardback book
Linen book cloth
Linocut
Suede
Edition of 10

British artist Toby Ziegler describes his relationship with books as visceral. 'I like the materials, textures and smells of books', he explains. For him, books carry two stories: one in the words themselves, and another in the creases, folds, scuff-marks and water stains that tell the story of the book as an object. 'My books evoke the times and places that I have read them, and hint at everyone else who has ever handled them.'

This artist's edition of *The Alienation of Objects*, the standard version of which was published to accompany an exhibition of Ziegler's work at the Zabludowicz Collection in London, was hand-bound by Ziegler himself. 'I wanted the books to feel pre-handled', he says. 'I also wanted them to feel like a mutation of a special binding, so I used traditional materials ... but in unconventional configurations.' To create the text for the cover, Ziegler first made a print from a linocut. This print was then scanned and foil-stamped into the linen.

—

PUBLISHER *Zabludowicz Collection, UK*
ART DIRECTION *Toby Ziegler, Yes*
DESIGN *Yes, Toby Ziegler, Elizabeth Johnson*
DATE *2010*

Toby Ziegler
The Alienation of Objects

Penguin
Drop Caps

||||||||||||||||||||||||||||||||

Specifications
Edge staining
Foil stamping
Hardback book
Spot colour

Penguin's Drop Caps is a series
of twenty-six hardback editions
of classic works of literature,
each of which features on its
cover a specially designed letter
of the alphabet by type designer
Jessica Hische. The project was a
collaboration between Hische and
Penguin art director Paul Buckley,
who introduced Hische's work to
Elda Rotor, editorial director of
Penguin Classics.

 Buckley began by drawing
up the basic series design, which
features a rainbow-hued spectrum
of colours across all twenty-six
titles, complete with matching

staining to the paper edges.
For each title, Hische designed
a custom drop cap based on the
content of the book. Buckley then
selected a colour scheme for the
drop cap and designed the other
cover elements to complement it.
While each front cover works in
its own right, the series takes on a
whole new dynamic when placed
on a bookshelf – spines out – in
A–Z order.
—

PUBLISHER *Penguin Group, USA*
CREATIVE DIRECTOR *Paul Buckley*
DESIGN *Jessica Hische, Paul Buckley*
TYPOGRAPHY *Jessica Hische*
DATE *2013*

B°Tong & EMERGE
Split LP

Specifications
Digital offset printing
Gloss varnish
Hand lettering
Hand-painted record sleeve
Marbled 12" vinyl record
Ready-made stencils
Solo Goya Triton acrylic paint
Stencil paint
Edition of 100

Founded in 2010, Attenuation Circuit is a German record label specializing in experimental music. This split LP by drone/ambient artists B°Tong and EMERGE is the first release in the label's Vinyl Series. While such traditional production techniques as screen printing are fairly common in the experimental music scene, Accentuated Circuit wanted to take things a step further. Each record in the Vinyl Series comes in an edition of 100, and each sleeve in that edition is hand-painted by artist Tine Klink. The names of the featured musicians are then stencilled on either side.

While no two sleeves in a particular release are the same, they all share a common colour scheme and style of painting. In the case of this first release in the series, Klink applied a feather to the bold stripes of blue and green acrylic paint to create an ornamental, 3D motif. Even the vinyl itself is unique: the manufacturing process used to create the marbled effect results in a different pattern with each pressing.

—

PUBLISHER *Attenuation Circuit, Germany*
ART DIRECTION *Gerald Fiebig, Sascha Stadlmeier*
COVER ARTWORK *Tine Klink*
INLAY CARD *Jens Börner*
DATE *2012*

Yeasayer
Fragrant World

||||||||||||||||||||||||||||||||||||||||

Specifications
2 'splatter' 12" vinyl records
Gatefold tip-on sleeve
Newsprint
Poster
Spot gloss UV varnish

Fragrant World is the third studio album by American psychedelic pop band Yeasayer. This double-vinyl edition features a gatefold tip-on sleeve, where the cover artwork is printed separately and then glued to the sleeve.

—

PUBLISHER *Mute, UK*
ART DIRECTION & DESIGN *Other Means*
PRODUCTION *Mute*
DATE *2012*

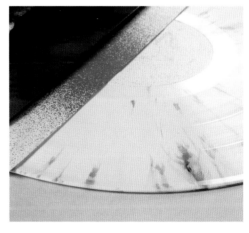

Junip
Junip

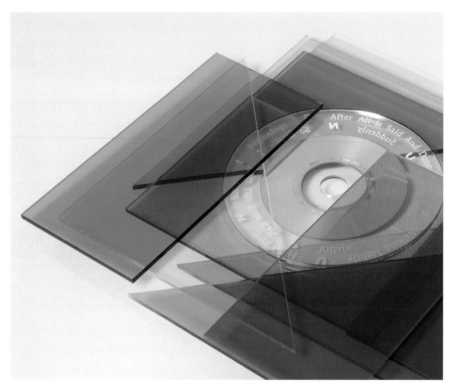

Specifications
2 CDs
Acrylic
Multi-panel case
White rubber bands
Edition of 400

According to José González, lead singer and guitarist with Swedish folk/psychedelic rock band Junip, the making of their second, self-titled studio album was far from easy. In fact, he suggests, nothing they do is ever straightforward. 'In our case, it's never simple. All the ups and downs', he adds, returning to the subject of the record, 'were very "Junip", so titling it with our name seemed appropriately iconic. It's truly a band album.'

This element of complexity has been carried over into the deluxe edition of the album, for which the band decided to discard the traditional concept of packaging and start from scratch. Nine coloured, geometrically cut acrylic panels slot together to encase two CDs. Once assembled, the jigsaw-like protective whole is held together by four white rubber bands. As its designer comments, 'It's not easy to handle, it's absolutely not practical, but, man, this looks amazing.'

—
PUBLISHER *City Slang, Germany*
ART DIRECTION & DESIGN *Zwölf*
DATE *2013*

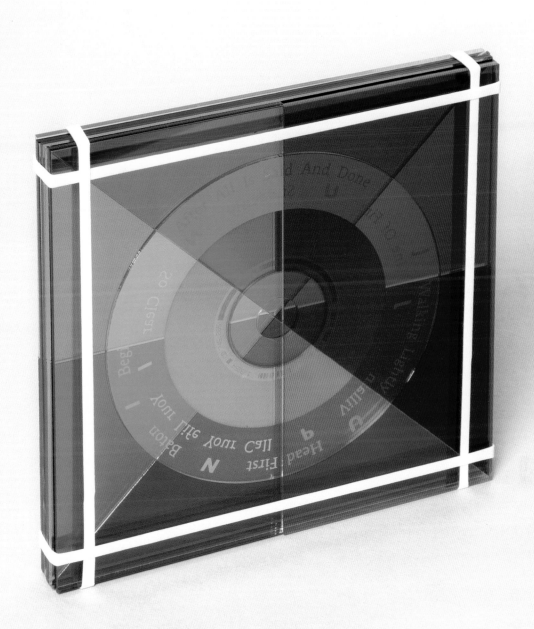

Gabby Young & Other Animals
The Band Called Out For More

||||||||||||||||||||||||||||||||||

Specifications
Box
CD
Colour wheel
Die cutting
Gold foil blocking
Spiral fold

For Gabby Young, lead singer of British 'circus swing' band Gabby Young & Other Animals, the packaging for the band's music is of particular importance. 'I always want to give our fans something they can treasure,' she explains, 'something that enhances the visual element of the music and that excites and inspires the listener.' The packaging for this, the special edition of the band's second album was a collaboration between Young, designer Andy Hau, photographer Gem Hall and graphic designers Kundalini Arts, all of whom brought something different to the project.

According to Hau, who has a background in architecture, everyone involved wanted the packaging to be a physical representation of the songs on the CD, something that the listener would immediately associate with the band: 'We wanted to capture the joy and exuberance in the music, as well as Gabby's unusual, dynamic and colourful persona on stage.' Taking as their inspiration a kaleidoscope, Hau and the others developed two pieces of packaging that could be interacted with by the user: a box with an integrated colour wheel and a spiral-fold sleeve for the CD.

As Young notes, 'I love to see the look on people's faces when they pick up this CD. It seems to fill them with childlike wonderment, and that's exactly what I wanted.'
—

PUBLISHER *Gift of the Gab Records, UK*
ART DIRECTION *Andy Hau, Gabby Young, Stephen Ellis*
DESIGN *Andy Hau*
PHOTOGRAPHY *Gem Hall*
ILLUSTRATION *Kundalini Arts*
DATE *2012*

Glasvegas
Later ... When the TV Turns to Static

|||||||||||||||||||||||||||||||

Specifications
Black foil stamping
Black Wibalin Finelinen
CD
DVD
Hardback book
White foil stamping
White ribbon

The zigzag motif that runs throughout the various editions of *Later ... When the TV Turns to Static* was the idea of James Allan, Glasvegas's guitarist and lead singer. In fact, according to Brian Wishart, the designer tasked with realizing the musician's ideas, Allan led the creative direction from the start, providing a wealth of ideas. Once the visual identity for the album – the band's third – had been decided, Allan and Wishart began work on the deluxe edition. It soon became clear to the both of them that it should take the form of a substantial piece of print.

The defining moment came when Allan showed Wishart a journal-style book by American film-maker David Lynch. This inspired them to create *The Glasvegas Almanac*, a forty-page hardback journal full of content about both the band and the album, including lyrics, tongue-in-cheek illustrations of each member of the band and photos of the group in the studio. The journal also acts as the packaging for a CD of the album itself and a specially recorded DVD of an acoustic performance of the entire record.

—

PUBLISHER *BMG, Germany*
ART DIRECTION *James Allan*
DESIGN *Brian Wishart (reflexblue), James Allan*
ILLUSTRATION *Brian Wishart*
PRODUCTION *Modo*
DATE *2013*

The Hunger
Issue 4

||||||||||||||||||||||||||||||||

Specifications
Diffuser foil
Hardback magazine
Matt lamination
Softback magazine

The Hunger is a biannual music, fashion, culture and lifestyle magazine created by the British portrait and fashion photographer John Rankin Waddell, aka Rankin. Collaborating with recognized and emerging talents, the magazine offers an alternative platform for self-expression to those working in the various creative industries.

The fourth issue of *The Hunger*, based on the theme of 'Girls, Girls, Girls', focuses on the work of six female stars of pop: Jessie J, Rita Ora, Iggy Azalea, Grimes, A*M*E and Gabrielle

Aplin. Each was chosen on account of her unique attitude towards the music industry.

The magazine's hand-scrawled logo – written by Rankin himself – is paired with discreet cover typography, allowing the photography to take precedence. An element of luxury is created through the use of diffuser foil, while matt lamination provides a more tactile reading experience. This approach is adopted throughout the internal pages, with a consistent type size used for both article titles and pull-out quotes, each printed in a silver

Pantone to differentiate them from the main text.

Accompanying the six softback editions of issue 4 (one cover for each featured pop star) was a limited-edition hardback featuring the American fashion model Crystal Renn. The change in format was intended to lend the magazine the look and feel of a collectible book.

—

PUBLISHER *Hunger Publishing Ltd, UK*
CREATIVE DIRECTOR *Vicky Lawton*
SENIOR DESIGNER *Calum Crease*
JUNIOR DESIGNER *Tom Etherington*
PHOTOGRAPHY *Rankin*
DATE *Spring/Summer 2013*

||||||||||||||||||||||||||||||||

Specifications
2 clear 12" vinyl records
Die cutting
Spot colour
Edition of 250

While looking for someone to create the artwork for *Corollaries*, Ukrainian composer and pianist Lubomyr Melnyk's first release for Erased Tapes, the record label's Sofia Ilyas stumbled across the work of American artist Gregory Euclide. It soon became clear that his style of painting resonated with Melnyk's multilayered and 'continuous' style of music. Contact was made, and Euclide quickly created two paintings – each measuring 123 × 123 cm (48 × 48 in.) – while listening to early mixes of the recordings on repeat. Euclide describes his interpretation of *Corollaries* as 'a continuous cycle of growth and decay'.

It was important to both Euclide and label founder Robert Raths that the listener's discovery of Melnyk's music should begin with the various components of the packaging. To reflect the importance of improvisation and chance to Melnyk's continuous music, Euclide used the outline of a crumpled shopping bag for the die cut on the outer sleeve. Inside, the two printed inner sleeves carry Euclide's paintings; once removed, they also reveal the lyrics to the opening song. Finally, the listener arrives at the records themselves and the extraordinary music they hold.

—

PUBLISHER *Erased Tapes, UK/Germany*
ART DIRECTION & DESIGN *Gregory Euclide, Robert Raths, Sofia Ilyas*
ILLUSTRATION *Gregory Euclide*
PRODUCTION *The Vinyl Factory*
DATE *2013*

Lubomyr Melnyk
Corollaries

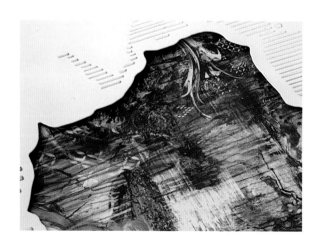

Berlin-based producer and musician Sascha Ring, aka Apparat, recorded the majority of *The Devil's Walk* in Mexico. It was only natural, therefore, that the cover art should feature some Mexican influences. Ring was particularly interested in the work of José-Guadalupe Posada, a nineteenth-century printmaker and draughtsman from Mexico, and so the illustrations for the cover were adapted to reflect Posada's style of drawing.

It was Ring's record label, Mute, who suggested a deluxe edition of the album. This gave the designers the scope to produce a real collector's item, something using specialist print techniques and high-quality materials. They soon landed on the idea of a CD sleeve in the form of a twenty-four-page hardback book.

The designers were keen to give the graphics a modern touch. Knowing that Ring was a fan of bright colours, they decided to use a pink metallic foil to emphasize the difference between old and new, and to create a physical contrast with the uncoated board used for the cover of the book. To accentuate this tactile element, the foil was blocked into the cover. This, according to the designers, was the icing on the cake.

—

PUBLISHER *Mute, UK*
ART DIRECTION & DESIGN
Carsten Aermes, Sascha Ring
ILLUSTRATION *Hanna Zeckau*
PRODUCTION *Mute*
DATE *2011*

Apparat
The Devil's Walk

||||||||||||||||||||||||||||||||||||||||||||||||||||||||||||||||||||||||||||

Specifications
CD
Foil blocking
Hardback book
Pink metallic foil
Uncoated board

Atoms for Peace
Amok

Amok is the debut album by Atoms for Peace, the experimental rock band featuring Radiohead's Thom Yorke. The artwork for the album, which was released in multiple formats, including a triple-gatefold vinyl edition (opposite and below) and a screen-printed box set (right), was created by long-time Radiohead collaborator Stanley Donwood. It consists of an apocalyptic vision of Los Angeles created from an original linocut by Donwood.

The screen-printed box set was originally produced for an immersive pop-up experience titled 'The Atoms for Peace Drawing Room'. Part gallery, part shop and part 'hanging out' space, it offered for sale exclusive vinyl, posters and other curiosities, many of which were 'live printed' in the Drawing Room on a specially installed silk-screen printing press.

—

PUBLISHER *XL Recordings, UK*
ART DIRECTION & DESIGN *Phil Lee, Stanley Donwood*
ARTWORK *Stanley Donwood*
PRODUCTION *Think Tank Media*
DATE *2013*

Specifications
3 12" vinyl records
9 single-sided 12" vinyl records
Blind embossing
Etched vinyl
Lift-off-lid box
Screen printing
Silver foil
Triple-gatefold record sleeve

Bleep
North/South/East/West

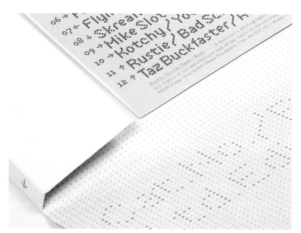

|||||||||||||||||||||||||||||||||

Specifications
16 photographic prints
CD
Die cutting
Fluorescent ink
Hand-assembled
Hand-numbered
Metallic-silver ink
Poster
Screen printing
Uncoated board
Edition of 100

North/South/East/West is the result of a musical, photographic and design project intended to highlight the electronic music of four different regions of the world: the north and south of the United Kingdom, and the east and west coasts of America. Two limited editions were produced, including this super-limited version.

The designers wanted the packaging to reflect the quality of the material it contained. This led to the use of coloured paper stocks and special inks for the outer wallets. They also created a custom typeface based on the four cardinal points of a compass.

—

PUBLISHER *Bleep, UK*
ART DIRECTION *Give Up Art*
DESIGN *Stuart Hammersley, Give Up Art*
PHOTOGRAPHY *Shaun Bloodworth*
PRODUCTION *Tadberry Evedale*
DATE *2010*

Specifications
Booklet
Embossing
Orange 12" vinyl record
Postcard
Poster
Slip case
Thread sewing
Edition of 250

This deluxe limited edition of *These Walls of Mine*, a highly personal album by American singer-songwriter Peter Broderick, was a collaboration between Broderick himself, Robert Raths of Erased Tapes and graphic designer Torsten Posselt of Berlin-based design studio Feld. The songs on the album started life as a series of spontaneous recordings, which Broderick initially posted online. Their inspirations were personal notes, Dictaphone ramblings, comments from fans and even an email from Broderick's father telling him that his beloved cat had gone missing.

This feline motif appears elsewhere in the design. In the booklet, a number of photographs of cats provide a visual narrative, while Broderick's drawing of his own cat appears on the inside of the gatefold sleeve. The outside of the sleeve features a self-portrait of Broderick taken with a disposable underwater camera; half of his face is covered by water. The title of the album led to the idea of a slip case – a container in which to store Broderick's innermost thoughts, cat pictures and drawings.

—

PUBLISHER *Erased Tapes, UK/Germany*
ART DIRECTION *Torsten Posselt,*
Peter Broderick, Robert Raths
GRAPHIC DESIGN *Torsten Posselt (Feld)*
PHOTOGRAPHY *Peter Broderick*
ILLUSTRATION *Peter Broderick*
PRODUCTION *The Vinyl Factory,*
Pinguin Druck
DATE *2012*

Peter Broderick
These Walls of Mine

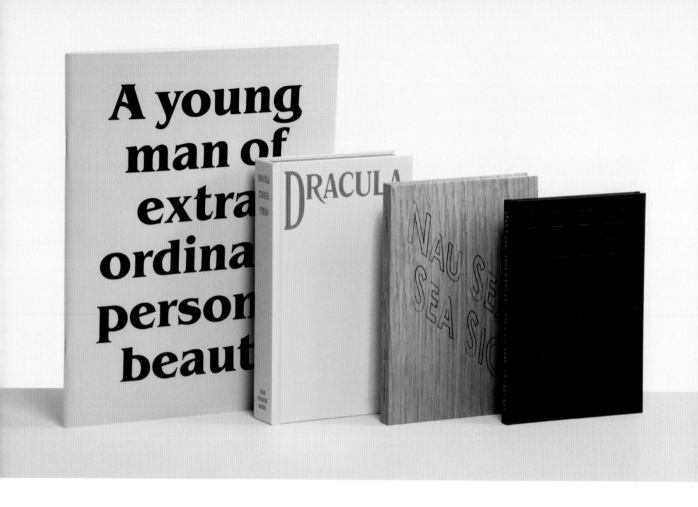

Four Corners
Familiars Series

For each book in the Familiars Series, a contemporary artist is asked to choose a classic work of fiction and illustrate it. Most importantly, however, they are asked to push the boundaries of what illustration can be. Each book is then designed to reflect the artist's approach and the book's theme or content. A total of eight books have been published so far, with more in the pipeline.

The design of *The Picture of Dorian Gray*, the first book in the series, was the idea of its illustrator, Gareth Jones. Jones was aware that Oscar Wilde's novel had first appeared in the July 1890 edition of *Lippincott's Monthly Magazine*, and so the illustrations are all advertisements (for Gitanes cigarettes), and each chapter is announced by a headline rather than a chapter heading.

The yellow-and-red colour scheme used for Bram Stoker's *Dracula* (1897), illustrated by James Pyman, is borrowed from the first British edition. The overall design includes various nods to the late 1890s, including the choice of typefaces (each character has his or her own font):

all were in use at the time of the book's first publication.

Kay Rosen's images for *Nau Sea Sea Sick*, a collection of sea stories by such writers as Katherine Mansfield and Stephen Crane, are about reflection. To emphasize the mirroring that goes on between the images, the book was bound using French folds. This technique also allowed the publishers to print much closer to the fore-edge than would normally be possible, and to have a large gutter margin.

For *Blumfeld, an Elderly Bachelor*, an unfinished story

by Franz Kafka first published in the 1930s, artist David Musgrave suggested a small format. Subsequent research showed that Kafka liked books of this size, with relatively large type, so these attributes were adopted for the Familiars edition. Kafka's story is about mysterious, unexplainable objects, and the Four Corners book, with its blind-debossed cover, is something of a mysterious object itself.

The format and materials used for Gustave Flaubert's *Madame Bovary* (1856) suggest high fashion magazines and the

luxurious, perhaps even decadent side to the book's heroine. They also refer to *The World of Interiors* (2006), a book by *Bovary*'s illustrator, Marc Camille Chaimowicz. The typeface, based on nineteenth-century French examples, was specially cut by type designer Charles Mazé.

The pink-and-green cover of *Vanity Fair* (1847–48) is based on a description of some stationery belonging to William Makepeace Thackeray's (anti-)heroine, Becky Sharpe. Moreover, the typefaces used in the book, Perpetua and Felicity, and the paper, Pamo, all

have female names. Two ribbons allow the reader to bookmark a place in the text and one of Donald Urquhart's images.

A Stick of Green Candy contains short stories by Denton Welch and Jane Bowles. Although both writers had their heydays in the 1940s, the cover harks back to the classic Faber covers of the 1950s. Colter Jacobsen's images are about pairs and reflections, so the back cover repeats the front. The high-gloss spine evokes the subject of the book's title.

For the cover of *The Prisoner of Zenda*, novelist and playwright

Anthony Hope's classic story of mistaken identity first published in 1894, the publishers used a printed and holographic version of the same book plate to play with the idea of copies and genuine articles. The small format was the suggestion of the book's illustrator, Mireille Fauchon, who had the idea of using late nineteenth- and early twentieth-century travel guides as a reference point.
—

PUBLISHER *Four Corners Books, UK*
SERIES DESIGN *John Morgan*
PRODUCTION *Martin Lee*
DATE *2007–*

Annual
Issue 5

||||||||||||||||||||||||||||||||||||||||||||||||||||||||||||||

Specifications
Foil stamping
Hardback magazine

For the fifth issue of *Annual*, a contemporary art magazine with a book-like format, the editors decided to ask five contemporary artists to produce five different limited-edition covers. The intention was for the magazine to appeal to collectors, to feel almost like an artwork in itself. The concept also chimed with the content of the fifth issue, which was based on artists' contributions in the form of writings, portfolios and interviews.

Working in collaboration with the editorial team, the five selected artists were given carte blanche, with each developing their own approach to the brief. The results embrace a range of media, including photography, collage and typography. This diversity is also what unifies the different covers, which have considerable visual impact when seen together.

Each design was allowed to fill the entire cover, with the only other text being the magazine logo, which was foil-stamped on both the front and the spine. To emphasize the magazine's similarity to a book, the covers were printed on an embossed Fedrigoni paper, Imitlin, which imitates the feel of linen. Only 200 copies of each cover were printed, making the magazine even more collectible.

—

PUBLISHER *APC Trading, France*
ART DIRECTION & DESIGN
Thibault Caizergues (Atlantique Studio)
COVER ARTWORK *Tom Burr, Annette Kelm, Sarah Morris, Kelley Walker, Lawrence Weiner*
PRODUCTION *Grafiche SIZ*
DATE *2012*

Modeselektor
Monkeytown

||||||||||||||||||||||||||||||||||||||||||||

Specifications
2 clear 12" vinyl records
Debossing
Hand-numbered
Hand-signed
Hardback book
Slip case
Edition of 500

Monkeytown is the third studio album by German electronic music outfit Modeselektor. Included in this deluxe limited edition of the album is a hardback book featuring unseen and exclusive photographs of the group on tour and in the studio. Each of the 500 copies of the book has been signed and numbered by Modeselektor themselves.
—

PUBLISHER *Monkeytown Records, Germany*
ART DIRECTION & DESIGN *Pfadfinderei*
PHOTOGRAPHY *Szary (Modeselektor)*
ILLUSTRATION *Pfadfinderei*
DATE *2011*

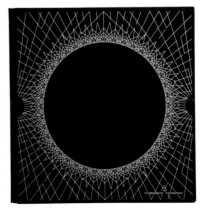

Cat Power
Sun

|||||||||||||||||||||||||||||||||

Specifications
Clear 7" vinyl record
Clear 12" vinyl record
Embossing
Gold foil board
Gold foil stamping
Matt lamination
Rigid board
Wide-spine sleeve

According to designer Matt de Jong, both he and Chan Marshall, aka Cat Power, were determined that this special edition of *Sun* should be as luxurious as possible. The album, Cat Power's ninth, is based around the themes of joyful experimentation, rebirth and self-sufficiency, so an Egyptian theme seemed appropriate. On the cover, gold foil against a matt-black background creates the perfect contrast between high and low shine. Inside, a foil-covered sleeve with embossed hieroglyphics contains the 7" record, which features unreleased tracks. It was felt that, in addition to beautiful packaging, a true deluxe edition should also include unheard material. Finally, clear vinyl has been used throughout to reiterate both the exclusivity and the simple beauty of the package.

—

PUBLISHER *Matador Records, USA*
ART DIRECTION & DESIGN *Matt de Jong*
ILLUSTRATION *Chan Marshall*
TYPOGRAPHY *Matt de Jong*
PRODUCTION *A to Z Media*
DATE *2012*

||||||||||||||||||||||||||||||

Specifications
2 CDs
Cardboard
DVD
Gloss lamination
Hardback book

This special edition of *Queen of the Wave*, the fourth album by Finnish musical collective Pepe Deluxé, is presented in the form of a sixty-four-page book. Inside the book is an expanded version of the album, which is described by the band as an 'esoteric pop opera in three parts'. The story of the opera is based on *A Dweller on Two Planets* (1905), Frederick S. Oliver's bizarre and posthumously published account of life in a technologically advanced Atlantis.

The album, which took four years to make, features sixty-three musicians from three different continents and some very unusual 'instruments'. These include Thomas Edison's ghost-hunting machine and the Great Stalacpipe Organ in Luray Caverns, Virginia, officially the largest musical instrument in the world. Further details about the album's making are contained in the highly illustrated book. 'It looks so crazy', observes Pepe Deluxé's Paul Malmström. 'It looks as the album sounds. Too much of everything, but in a good way.'

—

PUBLISHER *Catskills Records, UK*
ART DIRECTION *James Spectrum*
DESIGN *James Spectrum, Vilunki 3000*
ILLUSTRATION *James Spectrum*
PRODUCTION *DL Imaging, Toppan Leefung*
DATE *2012*

Pepe Deluxé
Queen of the Wave

Flying Lotus
Until the Quiet Comes

Specifications
2 12" vinyl records
Embossing
Gatefold sleeve
Tipped-on artwork

Until the Quiet Comes is the fourth studio album by American electronic producer Flying Lotus. The album draws on a wide range of influences, including African percussion, psychedelia and the human subconscious. The album's dream-like musical narrative is reflected in the underwater photography that forms the basis of the artwork. For this special edition, the cover image was printed separately before being attached to the buckram-covered gatefold sleeves.

—

PUBLISHER *Warp, UK*
ART DIRECTION *Stephen Serrato, B+*
DESIGN *Stephen Serrato*
PHOTOGRAPHY *B+, Dan Kitchens*
PRODUCTION *James Burton (Warp)*
DATE *2012*

Woody & Paul
Heroes and Zeroes

|||||||||||||||||||||||||||||||||||||||||||||||||||||||||||||||||

Specifications
12" vinyl record
28 unique sleeves
Bullet holes
Grey board
Screen printing
Unique Polaroid photo

For the vinyl edition of *Heroes and Zeroes*, Woody Veneman, singer and guitarist with Dutch band Woody & Paul, invited each of his favourite illustrators to design a cover. In the end, twenty-eight illustrators, both amateur and professional, participated in the project. Each cover was limited to nine or ten copies, and was screen printed by the band.

According to Veneman, the project was a reaction to the soulless and anonymous nature of mass production. It was also intended to reflect the band's DIY ethic and alternative sound. One sleeve resembles a target used in shooting practice. On closer inspection, it becomes clear that both the sleeve and the record inside are sporting a bullet hole.
—

PUBLISHER *Quadrofoon Records, The Netherlands*
ART DIRECTION *Woody Veneman*
COVER ARTWORK *Wolf Aartsen, Josine Beugels, Melle de Boer, Myrte Coemans, Michiel Corten, Vincent Dams, Jan Doms, Maarten Donders, Thom Dubé, Jeroen Erosie, Darko Groenhagen, Paul van Hulten, Joshua van Iersel, Rik van Iersel, Teun Jansen, Lucas Maassen, Johan Moorman, Richard Nijhuis, Geert Oosterhof, Peter van de Riet, Erik Sjouerman, Erwin Thomasse, Peer Veneman, Woody Veneman, Bart Waalen, Pieter Wels, Hans de Wit*
PRODUCTION *Woody Veneman*
DATE *2011*

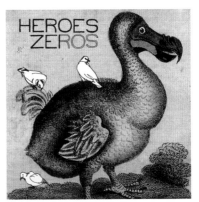

Unoiki
Uno-Iki-San

|||||||||||||||||||||||||||||||||

Specifications
2 CDs
Fold-out poster wallet
Hand-assembled
Hand-numbered
Edition of 100

Consisting of sixteen tracks spread over two CDs, *Uno-Iki-San* was launched to celebrate the third anniversary of Unoiki, a self-styled 'exploratory platform' for electronic music and related visual art. Four different designs were created for the packaging, which was the result of several months of research. Highly economical and ecological, it consists of an A3 sheet of 300-gsm card that has been folded to hold the CDs; once unfolded, it becomes a poster. According to Unoiki, the concept behind the packaging was for the listener to be presented with a 'floating' CD, suspended within the folded card.
—

PUBLISHER *Unoiki Collective Label Network, Germany*
ART DIRECTION & DESIGN *Jonathan Mangelinckx*
PHOTOGRAPHY *Jonathan Mangelinckx*
PRODUCTION *ABC Europe*
DATE *2013*

Novum
Issue 11/11

||||||||||||||||||||||||||||||||

Specifications
Die cutting
Magazine
Offset printing

The November 2011 issue of German graphic design magazine *Novum* was published with six differently coloured versions of the cover, the product of 48,000 passes through a printing press. Most significantly, however, each cover had been subjected to 104 extremely detailed die cuts. The result, according to *Novum*, is a 'metamorphosis of paper', inspired by the geodesic domes of American architect and designer Richard Buckminster Fuller.

—

PUBLISHER *Stiebner Verlag GmbH, Germany*
CREATIVE DIRECTION *Max Kuehne*
ART DIRECTION *Oliver Klyne*
DESIGN *Max Kuehne, Carolin Rauen*
PHOTOGRAPHY *Michael Pfeiffer*
PRODUCTION *Printarena, Paperlux*
DATE *2011*

Penguin
Clothbound Classics

Specifications
Book cloth
Hardback book
Matt foil stamping

Coralie Bickford-Smith, the designer behind the Clothbound Classics series, saw the project as an opportunity to create 'beautiful, timeless artefacts for people to enjoy, cherish and pass on'. Inspired by type designer Ruari McLean's books on Victorian bindings, Bickford-Smith set out to create sumptuous, tactile books – each one a new edition of a classic work of literature – that evoke a rich heritage of bookbinding while remaining appealing to modern readers. The design of each book is based on an object that is central to the tale within; this object is also intended to arouse curiosity in both new and existing readers of that book. As Bickford-Smith notes, 'As we approach an age where e-books become the natural heir to the cheap paperback, there seems to be a growing market for something at the other end of the scale that celebrates the tactile qualities of print.'

—
PUBLISHER *Penguin Books, UK*
ART DIRECTION & DESIGN *Coralie Bickford-Smith, Jim Stoddart*
ILLUSTRATION *Coralie Bickford-Smith, Despotica*
PRODUCTION *Rita Matos, Clays Ltd*
DATE *2008-13*

Wilco
The Whole Love

|||||||||||||||||||||||||||||

Specifications
2 12" vinyl records
10" vinyl record
Book cloth
Die cutting
Rigid board
Slip case with inner box

The Whole Love is the eighth album by American rock band Wilco, and the first for the group's own label, dBpm. To reflect the nature of the music, drawings by American abstract expressionist artist Joanne Greenbaum were used throughout the special edition. Of particular importance to the overall design is a balance between the complexity of the illustrations and open space; this is carried over into the design of the booklets, where restrained typography and openness on the page give more space to the artwork. The die-cut holes in the cover provide a glimpse of the illustrations on the inner sleeves.
—

PUBLISHER *dBpm Records, USA*
ART DIRECTION *Jeff Tweedy,*
Lawrence Azerrad (LADdesign)
DESIGN *Lawrence Azerrad*
PHOTOGRAPHY *Mikael Jorgensen*
ILLUSTRATION *Joanne Greenbaum*
DATE *2011*

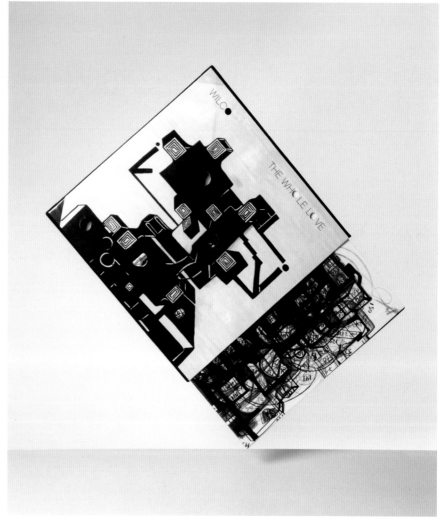

Woodkid
The Golden Age

||||||||||||||||||||||||||||||

Specifications
Black Brillianta canvas
CD
Foil stamping
Gilt-edged paper
Hardback book

For the special edition of the debut album by French director and singer-songwriter Yoann Lemoine, aka Woodkid, the record label wanted to create an object that people would be eager to open, read, listen to, close, reopen and ultimately keep. The result was a hardback book containing a CD of the album and a story by Woodkid constructed around the album's songs.

Since many of the themes of the story are of a timeless nature – childhood, innocence, love, but also growth, pain and violence – the book was made to resemble a Bible or prayerbook; the record label also liked the idea of a cold and forbidding exterior contrasted with a warm and inviting interior. Canadian-born artist Jillian Tamaki was approached to illustrate the book, based on Woodkid's descriptions of the story and the album's lyrics. It is this blending of the visual and the musical that is at the heart of the project.

—

PUBLISHER *Green United Music, France*
ART DIRECTION *Woodkid, Pierre Le Ny*
ART EDITOR *Julie Politi*
ILLUSTRATION *Jillian Tamaki*
PRODUCTION *ADM, Paris*
DATE *2013*

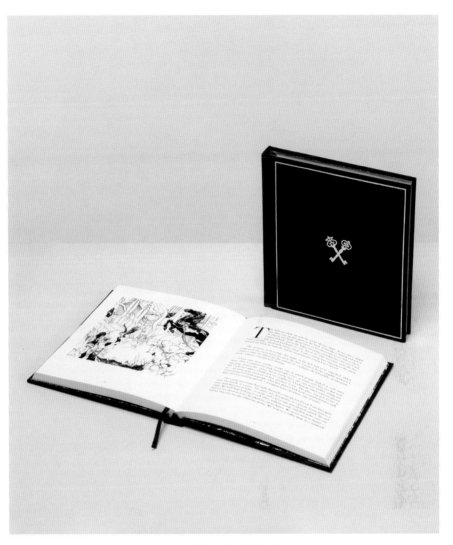

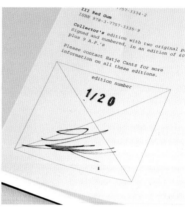

Jacqueline Hassink
The Table of Power 2

||||||||||||||||||||||||||||||||||||

Specifications
2 photographic prints
3 cover options
Foil stamping
Hand-numbered
Hand-signed
Hardback book
Slip case
Wood (cherry, red gum, walnut)
Edition of 20 per cover option

In *The Table of Power 2*, Dutch photographer Jacqueline Hassink revisits a subject she first explored in the 1990s: the boardroom tables at the headquarters of some of the largest multinational corporations in the world. In particular, she wanted to find out if these centres of economic power in a post-industrial age had changed in the wake of the financial crash of 2008.

For this special edition of the book, designer Irma Boom devised three different wooden covers. 'I noticed that the tables are always wooden', she explains, referring to Hassink's photographs. 'There's hardly ever any cloth on them.' The accompanying text is set in Courier, to evoke the business world of a certain age, and each copy of the book comes with two photographic prints.

—
PUBLISHER *Hatje Cantz Verlag, Germany*
ART DIRECTION & DESIGN *Irma Boom*
PRODUCTION *Druckerei Grammlich*
DATE *2012*

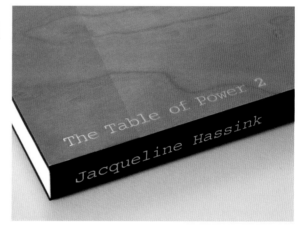

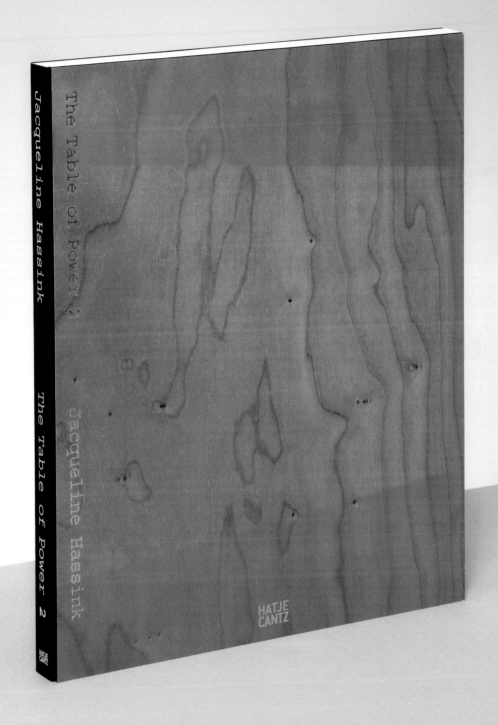

The Sochi Project
Sochi Singers

Specifications
2 photographic prints
Custom-made envelope
Hand-signed
Paperback book
Screen printing
Slip case
Edition of 25

Host to the 2014 Winter Olympics, the popular Black Sea resort of Sochi embodies two key aspects of modern Russia: respect for the country's cultural heritage and a growing taste for all things 'bling'. *Sochi Singers* explores how a deeply rooted Russian tradition – restaurants with live musicians singing songs to the seated diners – exists side by side with the city's newfound love of glamour.

In this special edition of the book, the two faces of Sochi are brought together in the form of extracts from the songs set in gold type. These extracts are too large for the page, but deliberately so, thereby symbolizing the loud snatches of song that can be heard from every restaurant as one takes a stroll along the Sochi boulevard.

—

PUBLISHER *The Sochi Project, The Netherlands*
ART DIRECTION *Rob Hornstra, Kummer & Herrman*
DESIGN *Kummer & Herrman*
PHOTOGRAPHY *Rob Hornstra*
DATE *2011*

Published to celebrate the twentieth anniversary of *Colors* magazine, 'Collector' is a special issue dedicated to people who collect, whether that be works of art or everyday objects. To reflect the way in which collectors are keen to preserve their items, the magazine was packaged in its own black or gold bubble-wrap envelope.

—

PUBLISHER *Fabrica Spa, Italy*
CREATIVE DIRECTION *Sam Baron*
ART DIRECTION *Magdalena Czarnecki, Brian Wood*
DESIGN *Namyoung An*
PRODUCTION *Mauro Bedoni, Grafiche Tintoretto*
DATE *2011*

Colors
Issue 79: Collector

|||||||||||||||||||||||||||||||||

Specifications
Bubble-wrap envelope
Foil blocking
Magazine
Sticker

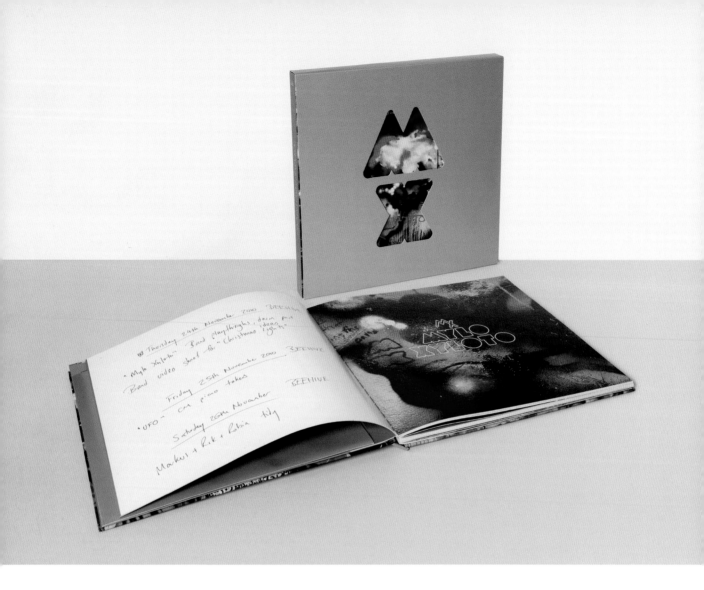

Coldplay
Mylo Xyloto

||||||||||||||||||||||||||||||

Specifications
12" vinyl record
CD
Die cutting
Hardback pop-up book
Metallic-silver ink
Poster
Spot UV varnish
Stickers and stencils

Central to the artwork for all formats of *Mylo Xyloto*, Coldplay's fifth studio album, was the construction of a large-scale graffiti wall. A collaboration between Coldplay and London-based design studio Tappin Gofton, the wall was subsequently painted by the band themselves under the watchful eye of British graffiti artist Paris. This process was documented on a daily basis by British photographer Kate Peters. The resulting plethora of images was used for sleeve artwork, for marketing materials and on the band's website.

For this deluxe vinyl edition of the album, Tappin Gofton worked closely with the band to design a hardback book featuring a centrepiece by American pop-up artist David A. Carter. As well as containing the 12" vinyl, the book houses such extras as a large fold-out poster of the graffiti wall.
—

PUBLISHER *Parlophone/EMI Records Ltd, UK*
ART DIRECTION & DESIGN *Tappin Gofton*
ART *Paris, Coldplay*
PHOTOGRAPHY *Kate Peters, Phil Harvey, Matthew Miller*
POP-UP DESIGN *David A. Carter*
PRODUCTION *Parlophone/EMI Records Ltd*
DATE *2011*

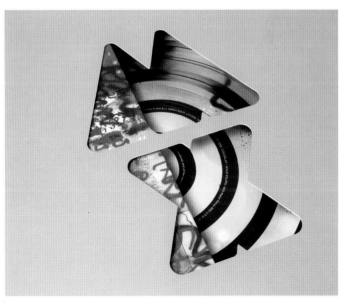

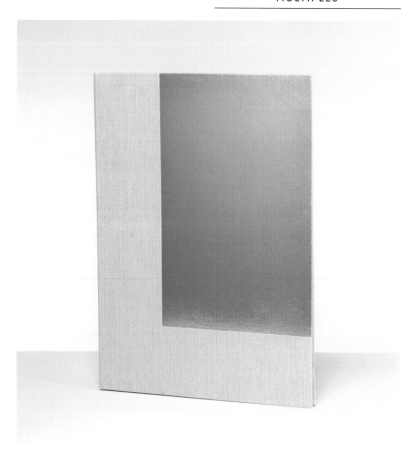

Lukas Wassmann
L

|||||||||||||||||||||||||||||||

Specifications
Gold leaf
Hand-bound
Hand-numbered
Hand-signed
Hardback book
Linen book cloth
Photographic print
Edition of 24

L is a selection of works by
Swiss photographer Lukas
Wassmann, chosen by publisher
Dino Simonett in collaboration
with the photographer. The large-
format book (48 × 33 cm/18⅞ ×
13 in.) comes in two editions: one
limited to 400 copies, the other –
shown here – to 24, with gold leaf
on its cover. The book has been
printed on glossy paper because,
says Wassmann, 'of sexiness'.

—

PUBLISHER *Edition Dino Simonett,*
Switzerland
ART DIRECTION *Dino Simonett*
DESIGN *Dino Simonett, Bruno Margreth*
PHOTOGRAPHY *Lukas Wassmann*
DATE *2012*

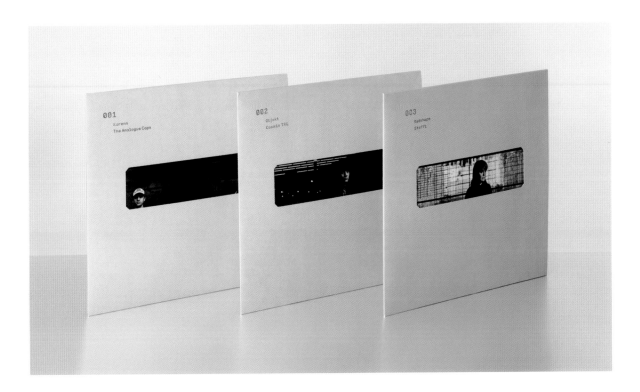

|||||||||||||||||||||||||||||||||||||||||||||||||||||||

Bleep
The Green Series

The limited-edition vinyl releases that make up 'The Green Series' are intended to showcase the work of leading British and German techno producers. To keep the cost of each release as low as possible while retaining the feel of a collectible series, a single, die-cut sleeve was printed on to which could be stamped each record's title and track information. The die cut would allow for a portion of the inner-sleeve artwork – a duotone version of the full-colour artist portrait included with each record – to be visible, thus differentiating one release from another. The outer sleeves are made from an uncoated stock, providing a visual and tactile contrast to the high-gloss varnish of the inner sleeves.

—

PUBLISHER *Bleep, UK*
ART DIRECTION *Give Up Art*
DESIGN *Stuart Hammersley, Give Up Art*
PHOTOGRAPHY *Shaun Bloodworth*
PRODUCTION *Disc Solutions*
DATE *2013*

Specifications
2 photographic prints
12" vinyl record
Colourization
Debossing
Die cutting
Hand-signed
Hand-stamped
High-gloss UV varnish
Uncoated board

Marc Romboy & Ken Ishii
Taiyo

||||||||||||||||||||||||||||||||

Specifications
3 12" vinyl records
4 spot colours
Cardboard
CD
Die cutting
Poster
Slip case

Taiyo (the Japanese for 'sun') is the first collaboration between German tech-house pioneer Marc Romboy and Japanese techno producer Ken Ishii. Berlin-based design studio Hort worked with German photographer Michael Kohls to develop a visual language that would form the basis of the art direction across all formats.

Central to the appearance of the limited-edition box set are the die cuts in both the outer and the inner sleeves and their relation to the photography. Their position is such that the missing piece of the sleeve becomes a key element of the overall design. According to Hort, the box set 'references music's physical medium and the techniques involved in its production'.

—

PUBLISHER *Systematic Recordings, Germany*
ART DIRECTION & DESIGN *Hort*
PHOTOGRAPHY *Michael Kohls, Bene Brandhofer*
DATE *2012*

Nieves
Zine Box

Specifications
18 zines
Photocopying
Edition of 20

Founded in 2001, Nieves is an independent publishing house specializing in artists' books and zines (from 'magazines'). First released in 2004, the annual zine box set contains all the zines published by Nieves in the previous year. The set comes wrapped in a poster featuring the covers of the zines inside.

—

PUBLISHER *Nieves, Switzerland*
ART DIRECTION & DESIGN
Benjamin Sommerhalder
ARTISTS *Josse Bailly, Sabina Baumann, Massimiliano Bomba, Olaf Breuning, Rob Churm, Misha Hollenbach, Chris Hopkins, Rob Lowe, Stefan Marx, Hayan Kam Nakache, Emmanuelle Pidoux, Andy Rementer, Allison Schulnik, Shoboshobo, Peter Sutherland, Michael Swaney, Emi Ueoka, Jen Uman, Jocko Weyland, Jessica Williams*
DATE *2012*

Bruce Gilden
Foreclosures

||||||||||||||||||||||||||||||||||||||||||||||||||

Specifications
Black canvas
Black thread
Blind embossing
Found postcard
Hand-numbered
Paperback book
Screen printing
Singer sewing
Slip case
White foil blocking
Edition of 500

In the wake of the subprime mortgage crisis of 2008, millions of Americans were forced to leave their homes. In *Foreclosures*, American photographer Bruce Gilden documents the devastating effects of foreclosure in some of the country's worst-hit communities. In a significant departure for Gilden, who is best known as a street photographer, the images in *Foreclosures* display a distinct lack of people. Despite this absence of faces, however, the book is profoundly human.

The format of the book was dictated by the format of the photographs. The special edition, numbers 1–100 of the 500 copies printed, comes in a black-canvas slip case featuring a black screen-printed Stars and Stripes – a political as much as an aesthetic decision. All 500 copies include a postcard found in one of the featured states; in the special edition, the postcard has been signed by Gilden.

—

PUBLISHER *Browns Editions, UK*
ART DIRECTION & DESIGN *Jonathan Ellery, Sateen Panagiotopoulou*
PHOTOGRAPHY *Bruce Gilden*
PRODUCTION *Pureprint Group*
DATE *2013*

Wallpaper*
Special Issue: Handmade

Specifications
30 unique covers
Magazine
Matt UV varnish

For the August 2012 'Handmade' issue of *Wallpaper*, the magazine commissioned dozens of leading designers to create a series of unique covers. Significantly, the magazine's readers were able to suggest their preferred designer and tweet them a brief. The results were posted on the magazine's website, where readers were able to select and personalize the cover of their choice.

The 'Handmade' issue was dedicated to the third annual *Wallpaper** 'Handmade' exhibition, held during the 2012 Milan Furniture Fair. The exhibition featured a range of specially commissioned items by some of the world's most respected designers, artists, craftsmen and manufacturers.

—

PUBLISHER *IPC Media, UK*
EDITOR-IN-CHIEF *Tony Chambers*
ART DIRECTION *Meirion Pritchard*
ART EDITOR *Sarah Douglas*
GOVER ART *A Practice for Everyday Life, Bibliothèque, Anthony Burrill, Margaret Calvert, David Carson, Jonathan Ellery, Laurent Fetis, Vince Frost & Giles Revell, Melvin Galapon, HelloVon, Tom Hingston, Hort, Trevor Jackson, Quentin Jones, James Joyce, Alan Kitching, Henrik Kubel, Peter Miles, Nigel Robinson, Rob Ryan, Studio Frith, Supermundane, Hiroshi Tanabe, Kam Tang & Wallzo & Paul A. Young, Daisy de Villeneuve, Sam Winston, Ian Wright*
DATE *2012*

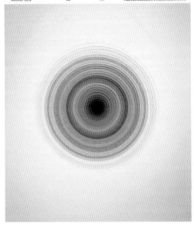

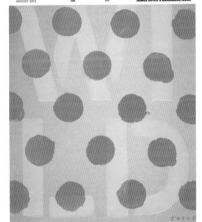

Quentin Blake
Beyond the Page

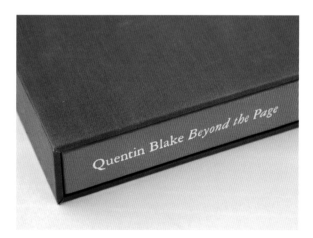

|||||||||||||||||||||||||||||||

Specifications
Book cloth
Gold foil blocking
Hand-signed
Hardback book
Ribbon
Slip case
Tipped-in page

In *Beyond the Page*, illustrator Quentin Blake looks back at a selection of his projects dating from 2000 onwards. To realize the book, Blake worked closely with Quentin Newark of London-based design studio Atelier Works. 'It's hard to imagine a better collaborator than Quentin Blake', says Newark. 'First he hands you a collection of the most delightfully crazy drawings, which are a job to design with, then he proves eminently flexible at the draft design stage.'

When it came to the special edition, explains Newark, all the design choices – the type of book cloth, the colour of the head and tail bands, the style of the endpapers – were derived from or related to Blake's drawings. 'We saw the design task as one of participation, quiet participation, to make everything that isn't his drawings subtle and controlled to highlight the exuberance of his pen and his brush.'

—

PUBLISHER *Tate Publishing, UK*
ART DIRECTION *Quentin Newark (Atelier Works)*
DESIGN *Daniela Meloni*
ILLUSTRATION *Quentin Blake*
PRODUCTION *DL Imaging, Toppan Leefung*
DATE *2012*

Moldover
Moldover

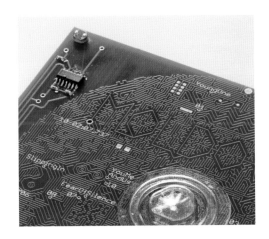

||||||||||||||||||||||||||||||||||

Specifications
556 timer
Analogue synthesizer
Battery
Capacitors
CD
Copper
Custom-printed circuit board
FR4 laminate
Hand-assembled
Headphone jack
LED
Photo-resistors
Resistors
Screen printing
Solder
Speaker
Switch

Otherwise known as the 'circuit-board CD', the special edition of the debut album by American musician and producer Moldover comes attached to a circuit board. Moreover, this circuit board is actually a 'light theremin', a musical instrument that allows you to alter the sound of a single note by moving your hand over one of two light sensors. The working electronics take up very little space, so the rest of the circuit board features a detailed maze (the solution to which is printed on the CD) and track information 'written' in circuitry.

—

PUBLISHER *Moldover, USA*
ART DIRECTION & DESIGN *Moldover*
ELECTRICAL ENGINEERING *Joe Martin*
PRODUCTION *Oasis CD, Gold Phoenix PCB*
DATE *2009*

Reel Art Press
The Rat Pack: Heritage Edition

Specifications

2 photographic prints
Ash veneer
Bespoke binding
Brillianta book cloth
Embossing
Hardback book
Laser etching
Magnetic closure
Orange foil blocking
Perspex window
Spot gloss UV varnish
Wooden box
Edition of 30

Consisting of a large number of unseen images, *The Rat Pack* is a photographic record of the legendary coterie of actors in their 1960s heyday. The large-format book (40 × 34 cm/15¾ × 13⅜ in.) was published in three limited editions. Of these, the 'Heritage' is the most exclusive. Contained in a handmade wooden box, it comes with two photographic prints, one of which is a rare vintage print from a selection of thirty.

The Heritage Edition was bound by hand, with particular attention given to the spine. This had to be strong enough to support the weight of the book block (all editions were printed in the United Kingdom), and flexible enough for the book to open and sit properly. For the box, several different prototypes were considered before a clean, simple wooden case was selected.
—

PUBLISHER *Reel Art Press, UK*
ART DIRECTION & DESIGN *Graham Marsh*
PHOTOGRAPHY *Gerald Smith*
PRODUCTION *Progress Packaging*
DATE *2010*

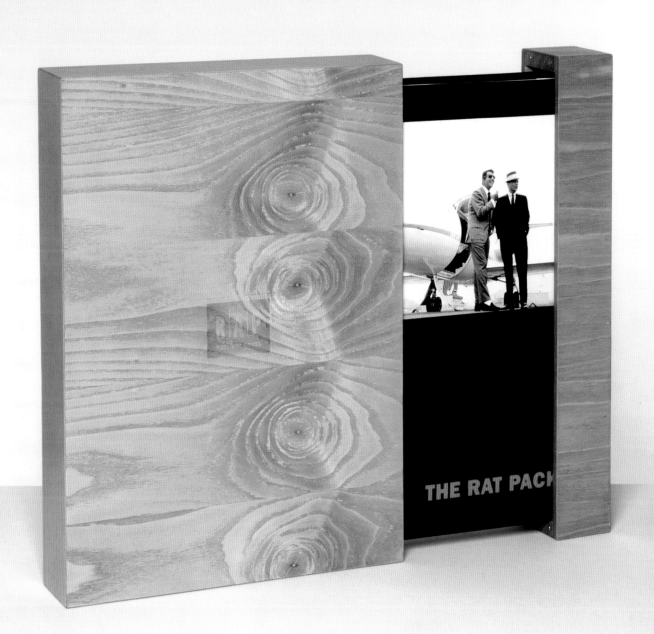

John Carpenter
The Fog

||||||||||||||||||||||||||||||

Specifications
2 clear 12" vinyl records
Art card
Gatefold tip-on sleeve
Matt lamination
Plastic overbag
Screen printing
Edition of 350

Founded by Spencer Hickman in 2011, Death Waltz Recording Company specializes in releasing remastered and repackaged soundtracks to classic and obscure horror films. For *The Fog* (1980) by John Carpenter, Hickman wanted to create a sleeve that would convey the atmosphere of the film even if it was not directly influenced by the film's imagery.

Introduced to Hickman via a friend, British artist Dinos Chapman, himself a lifelong horror fan, was commissioned to produce the artwork. The finished illustration, however, was presented on a piece of A4 paper, which meant that the image had to be carefully cropped. It was the project's designer, Tim Fowler, who suggested scanning the back of the paper and using it elsewhere on the gatefold sleeve, thereby creating a fully immersive item of packaging.

—

PUBLISHER *Death Waltz Recording Company, UK*
ART DIRECTION *Spencer Hickman, Tim Fowler*
DESIGN *Tim Fowler*
ILLUSTRATION *Dinos Chapman*
PRODUCTION *DMS Manufacturing*
DATE *2013*

||||||||||||||||||||||||||||||

Specifications
Detachable bookmark
Foil stamping
Hardback book

Penguin
F. Scott Fitzgerald Series

This series of new editions of F. Scott Fitzgerald's major works was published to mark the seventieth anniversary of the American author's death. Coralie Bickford-Smith's designs – a combination of ornate detail and mechanical-like repetition – are intended to evoke the elegance, glamour and modernity of the art deco period in which the books were written; the use of metallic foil also provides a tactile element. The front text panels continue the art deco theme and help to tie the series together.
—

PUBLISHER *Penguin Books, UK*
ART DIRECTION *Jim Stoddart*
DESIGN *Coralie Bickford-Smith*
PRODUCTION *Rita Matos*
DATE *2010*

HAND

Handmade, hand-manipulated and traditionally crafted
one-of-a-kind packaging and design

FUEL

INTERVIEW : MATTHEW LEE

PHOTOGRAPH : IVAN JONES

THE VINYL FACTORY

DINOS CHAPMAN

DINOS CHAPMAN is a British artist best known for his provocative collaborations with his brother, Jake. His first album, *Luftbobler* (2013; see page 152), was released by THE VINYL FACTORY, a London-based music and arts enterprise specializing in limited-edition vinyl. Its creative director, Sean Bidder, and Damon Murray of FUEL, the British design group responsible for *Luftbobler*'s unique hand-crafted aesthetic, joined Chapman to discuss how the project came together.

You've really pushed the boat out with the limited edition of *Luftbobler*. There's four-plate copper etching, five-colour screen printing, hand-etching on the record ... Was it all the result of collaboration?

Sean Bidder (SB): From a Vinyl Factory perspective, we've been totally open to ideas. It's been an open discussion.

Damon Murray (DM): We've been working with Dinos Chapman for more than ten years now, so it's a long relationship. We've always been drawn to a certain aesthetic – a slightly Soviet, pre-glasnost aesthetic. It's honest and utilitarian.

DM: The first conversation we had about this project was in St Petersburg. We were visiting the Russian Museum and looking at [Russian artist] Kazimir Malevich's paintings, and Dinos said, 'Ooh, they're good. That's a nice direction', and that was the start of it.

Dinos Chapman (DC): The design of the record mirrors the aesthetic of the music: clunky and handmade.

DM: Dinos had created his own world in the music, and we were trying to reflect that in the album design. Once we had decided on the aesthetic, we had to follow it through, from the inner sleeves to the labels on the physical records to the iTunes stuff and even the invitations for the launch party.

DC: It's just occurred to me where this record ideally would be bought: the record shop in *A Clockwork Orange*.

DM: There's an idealistic feel to both the design and the music. The music is idealistic, but it also sounds kind of wrong, and that's what we looked for in the design – something that has a theory behind it but the kind of theory that was abandoned years ago.

DC: The typeface is very constructivist, and the tape around the edges is very functional. It creates the feeling that it hasn't necessarily been put together by professionals with professional equipment. You can imagine a vast factory with dated machinery and old babushkas taping the edges. It's like something handed out by the Ministry of Information.

You can really feel the ink on this record …

DM: The ink is all matt. We were aiming to create all these tactile elements.

DC: At first we weren't sure what to put in that square at the centre of the cover.

DM: I designed the logo first because we needed to do that for the purposes of promotion. After that I knew the rest would follow. I put a placeholder in the middle for the etching.

DC: The original plan was for my brother to draw something, but he decided he didn't want to. Then I decided I liked the idea of a lonely, sad monster shambling around in the forest. The image we ended up using is a cropped section of a larger print of a teddy bear standing over a campfire and toasting a marshmallow, just as he's about to be eaten by a monster. It's the food chain – do you feel sorry for the marshmallow, the teddy bear or the monster? Personally, I feel most sorry for the monster.

SB: We worked with several different craftspeople on this project. The screen printing was done by K2 Screen in London, which has collaborated with a lot of artists, while the etching was done by the Paupers Press, also in London. These are companies who bring their own expertise and always deliver fantastic quality.

DM: The screen printing is just amazing. There's no overlapping.

DC: It's a very long process, but you have to take it slowly to be able to accommodate changes. When you slow a process down, you see what's working and what isn't. The final record is about two hundred steps away from our initial idea.

Were anyone's ideas rejected along the way?

DC: It was more a case of ideas being adjusted than ideas being rejected.

DM: We all knew our direction was correct, so it was more about developing that direction than narrowing down our ideas.

How does releasing a record made by a visual artist differ from releasing one made by somebody best known for making music?

SB: We discussed this a lot because it would have been very easy to say that it's a project by an artist so we'll put greater emphasis on the art side of things. But we were very much of the opinion that it should be released as a piece of music, and that it should be judged on that basis, rather than it being given special consideration because the musician had become well known in a different field.

DC: It's interesting to me that this record hasn't really been discussed in the art press. I don't know if they see it as purely a music release, but when we released it I thought I was going to be shot down in flames because of who I am, and I'm pleasantly surprised that I haven't been.

Was music originally just a hobby for you, Dinos?

DC: 'Hobby' isn't the right word. I like hobbies because that's when you do something purely for the love of doing it, but this became more serious than that. I've always fiddled around at the edges of the electronic music world, and at about the time Sean got in touch I knew I had to do something about it, rather than just continuing to amass more and more of this stuff that I was making.

SB: I'd heard that Dinos was making electronic music, and that interested me. I thought that, at the very least, it would be intriguing. I just started the conversation with him.

DC: I had at least 15 hours of stuff on my computers. I was surprised that Sean thought it was something worth investigating.

When The Vinyl Factory launched in 2001, online file-sharing was at its peak, CD sales were starting to decline and everybody was predicting the death of vinyl. Was starting the company a gamble?

SB: We looked at things in a different way. Vinyl in 2001 was relatively niche – as it is today – because the music industry was fixated on CDs. The industry didn't see a future in vinyl as a revenue-generator, but from the perspective of a small business with a global audience, it's appealing because there's a group of people who are incredibly passionate about vinyl. It's part of their culture so they'll help sustain it. Also, a lot of DJs were not about to stop using vinyl. Digital music is unsurpassable in terms of convenience and affordability, but now if you want a physical product it's got to be vinyl because of its sound quality, the artwork, its tactile nature and so on.

How important is art and design to The Vinyl Factory?

SB: It's really important to us that we don't just release music in a standard package. The music is the key component, but the artwork and design should also be special. When we started making limited editions, they weren't very common. We spent more money on production, making them look and feel as good as possible.

Is it the same audience buying vinyl today as it was ten years ago?

SB: It's definitely a younger audience now. Increasingly, there are only two ways of buying music: vinyl or digital. The number of people buying CDs is diminishing, and many young people want to start a collection, so they buy vinyl. There's a growing market for second-hand records, especially in the United States.

DC: I think people are bored of having a soundtrack to every moment of their daily lives, wandering around wearing headphones all the time. I can't do it any more. It's appealing for a short amount of time, but it's not a great way of listening to music. With a special object, you'll actually sit down and listen to the music.

SB: There's effort involved in getting up and putting on a record. Whenever we're doing several things at the same time, it devalues each of those experiences. And this is going to make me sound like an old man, but the sound of vinyl is part of the experience. We spent lots of time working on the sound quality of *Luftbobler*, collaborating with a mastering engineer to get the sound as good as possible. When it's processed and heard through an MP3 player, so much of it is lost. But when you master it and put it on a record, you can hear all the little nuances and details.

DC: Things like ghosts in the background that you hope are present when you're recording. Or deliberate decisions, like putting something way over in the corner, fluttering around. On a computer, you just can't hear that kind of thing.

SB: A lot of things put in the music can't be heard through computer speakers. It's the same with the quality of the artwork, the design: everything gets lost in a digital format.

DM: It's very hard to raise your game in terms of designing packaging when you're working with digital. But if you put all your energy into vinyl, you can really make it exceptional.

Is it necessary to release a record in various digital formats in order for it to get heard?

SB: We're really not anti-digital. Dinos's record is being released online and as a CD, and we're streaming it for free on SoundCloud, YouTube and elsewhere. We believe digital and vinyl can complement each other. We understand that there will always be a lot more people streaming music than buying it – that's the nature of the world right now. But there are still people buying records because of the quality of the sound and the design.

'We're really not anti-digital. Dinos's record is being released online and as a CD, and we're streaming it for free on SoundCloud, YouTube and elsewhere. We believe digital and vinyl can complement each other.'

DC: People are getting fed up with not owning anything physical. Digital music is a bit like CGI in films: for the first five years everybody thought it was the best thing ever, and now people are bored of it. A mobile phone is now everybody's favourite camera, although everyone's putting their images through filters to make them look like degraded black-and-white photos or Polaroids.

DM: It comes back to the idea of authenticity. Everything to do with vinyl is authentic.

DC: It's also about ownership. Giving somebody a vinyl album as a present is very different to 'gifting' them the same album online.

Who do you think is buying the limited edition *Luftbobler*?

SB: It's a bit dangerous thinking about who your audience is. You have to make what you want to make. In terms of The Vinyl Factory's limited editions, we have some relatively young collectors, some people who are obviously collectors, and then others who are interested and excited by individual projects.

Are any of you collectors?

DC: When I was young I collected stupid things. I collected conkers – I had a cupboard full of conkers. And one day I decided I didn't want to collect conkers any more, so I took them all and put them underneath a tree. It wasn't a conker tree, and I'd catch children throwing sticks up into this tree that wasn't a conker tree. I also collected stones with holes in them. I lived in Hastings in East Sussex, so I'd spend hours on the beach looking for stones with holes in them.

Were you bored as a kid?

DC: Totally. I had no friends!

Dinos Chapman, Sean Bidder and Damon Murray were photographed at The Vinyl Factory, Soho, London, UK

Dinos Chapman
Luftbobler

Specifications
3 180gsm 12" vinyl records
4-plate copper etching
5-colour screen printing
Black cloth
Clothbound gatefold sleeve
Debossing
Hand colouring
Hand etching
Hand-numbered
Hand-signed
Tipped-on artwork
Untreated cardboard
Edition of 300

The artwork for *Luftbobler*, the debut album by British artist Dinos Chapman, was inspired by a visit to the Russian Museum in St Petersburg. Accompanying Chapman was Damon Murray of FUEL, the London-based design group that created the artwork. 'We were given a tour of the museum,' explains Murray, 'and were struck by Kazimir Malevich's suprematist paintings. Dinos thought it would be nice if the design was along those lines.'

This double-vinyl limited edition features an etching by Chapman himself; hand-coloured and produced using four separate copper plates, it sits within a debossed panel on the front cover. The rest of the artwork has been screen-printed. 'By choosing to screen print on to heavy card,' says Murray, 'we retained a tactile quality that the original Malevich paintings have.'
—

PUBLISHER *The Vinyl Factory, UK*
ART DIRECTION & DESIGN
Damon Murray, Stephen Sorrell (FUEL)
ETCHING *Dinos Chapman*
PRODUCTION *K2 Screen, Paupers Press, The Vinyl Factory*
DATE *2013*

Very Nearly Almost
Issue 20

Specifications
Black and gold ink
Magazine
Screen printing

VNA, a street-art, illustration and art-culture magazine, has been producing limited-edition screen-printed covers since issue 10. Initially a marketing exercise, the use of such covers has since become a standard feature of every issue. Issue 20 was the first to be published with a second regular cover. In total, three versions were produced: a black-and-white design, for the high street; an online-only design, with black and gold ink; and the limited-edition screen-printed version, designed by Retna.

—

PUBLISHER *Very Nearly Almost Ltd, UK*
ART DIRECTION *Greg Beer*
DESIGN *Greg Beer, aron Darveniza, Aaron Griffiths, Rhys Atkinson*
COVER ART *Retna*
SCREEN PRINTING *White Duck Screen Printing*
DATE *2012*

The Machine
RedHead

~~~~~~~~

Specifications
3 12" vinyl records
CD
Foam
Gold spray paint
Hand-numbered
Lift-off-lid box
Watercolour
Edition of 50

According to DJ and producer Matt Edwards, aka The Machine, the concept behind the limited-edition reissue of *RedHead* was 'to take the recorded music and visual elements into the unknown and present a product that had never been made before'. The result was an extremely large handmade box – at 63 × 63 cm (24¾ × 24⅜ in.), the box is four times the size of a 12" – featuring hand-finished artwork by Australian artist Misha Hollenbach.

Working alongside Edwards to create the packaging for *RedHead* was James Masters, co-founder (with Edwards) of record label Rekids, and designer Joel Richards. One of Richards's tasks was to devise the typography and graphics. 'A large part of the visual work was done by Hollenbach's images,' he explains, 'so it was just a case of choosing a relevant typeface [while] trying to keep the graphics fairly minimal and unobtrusive.'

—

PUBLISHER *Pyramids of Mars under license from Rekids, UK*
ART DIRECTION *Matt Edwards, James Masters*
DESIGN *Joel Wells*
ILLUSTRATION *Misha Hollenbach (Perks and Mini)*
PRODUCTION *Modo*
DATE *2013*

Beacon
TWWS

~~~~~~~~~~~~

Specifications
Coloured 12" vinyl record
Certificate of authenticity
Epoxy and sugar (100% archival)
Hand-numbered
Hand-signed
Edition of 20

TWWS is the deluxe vinyl edition of *The Ways We Separate*, the debut album by American duo Beacon (Thomas Mullarney III and Jacob Gossett). Of particular note is the highly sculptural box in which the album is packaged. Handmade by Brooklyn-based sculptor Fernando Mastrangelo, each box is cast from a mixture of epoxy and sugar. 'To make the box', explains Mastrangelo, 'I had the letters milled into a piece of wood, which allowed me to make a wood prototype of the entire case. I then made a silicone mould of the wood prototype and began the casting process.' Such an unusual form of packaging is nothing new to Beacon's record label, Ghostly, which has been experimenting with various forms of music delivery, beginning with USB sticks, for a number of years.
—

PUBLISHER *Ghostly International, USA*
ART DIRECTION *Fernando Mastrangelo, Beacon*
DESIGN *Fernando Mastrangelo*
ALBUM DESIGN *Michael Cina*
ILLUSTRATION *Langdon Graves*
PRODUCTION *Fernando Mastrangelo*
DATE *2013*

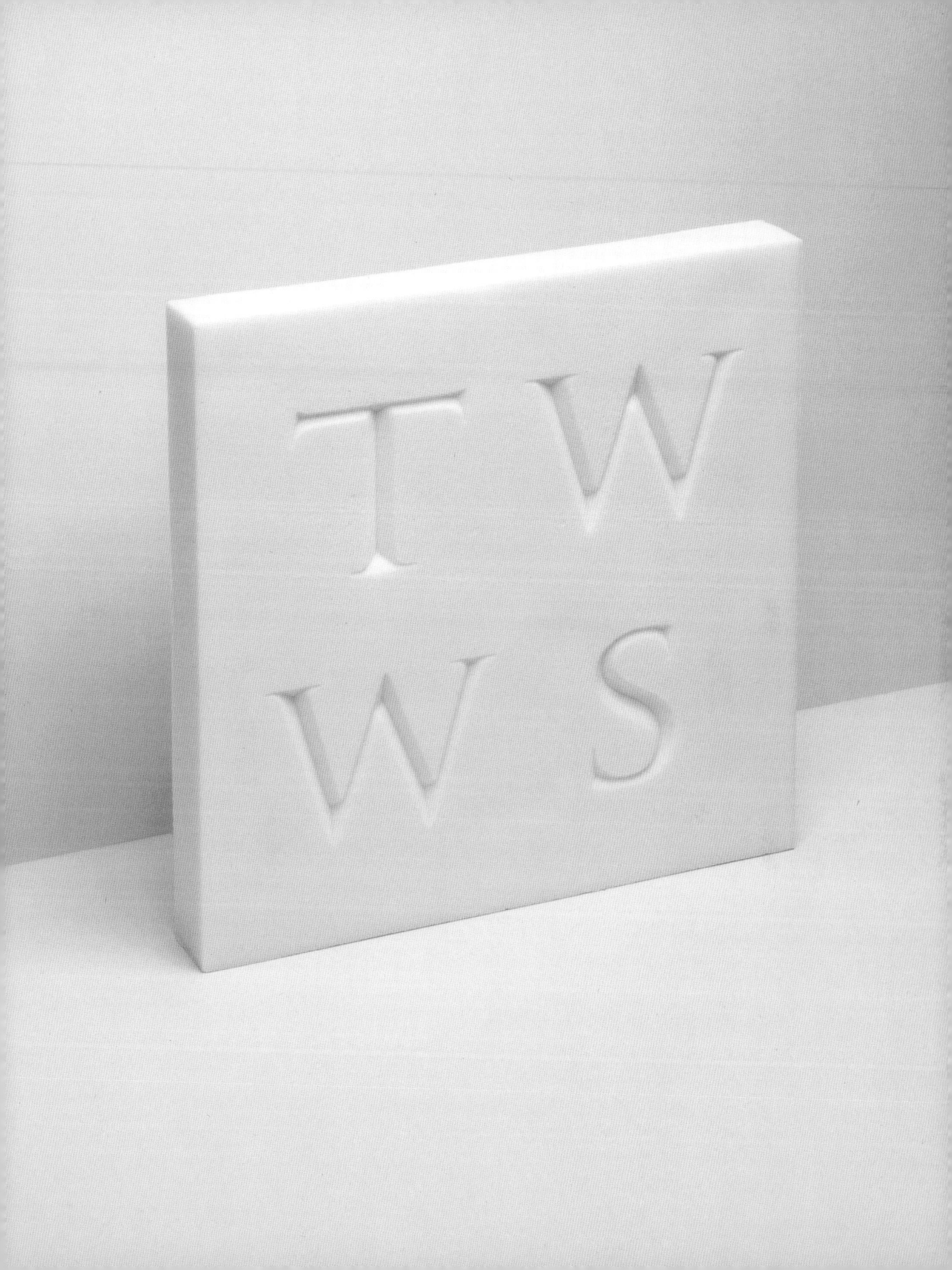
T W
W S

UC.Quarterly
Issue 1

Specifications
Letterpress printing
Magazine
Newsprint
Reclaimed test sheets
Rubber band
Rubber stamps
Saddle stitching
Screen printing

UC.Quarterly is a three-monthly summary of the most interesting projects to have appeared on the various blogs run by American graphic-design enterprise UnderConsideration. The insides of each magazine are printed by Newspaper Club, an online newspaper-creation and -printing service, while the covers are made from test prints and make-ready sheets reclaimed from various printers. These are then rubber-stamped by hand and 'bound' to the text with a thick rubber band.
—

PUBLISHER *UnderConsideration, USA*
ART DIRECTION & DESIGN *Armin Vit*
DATE *2013*

Martin Creed
Love to You

~~~~~~~~~~~~~~~~~~~~~~~~~~~~

Specifications
12" vinyl record
Gloss UV varnish
Hand-numbered
Hand painting
Hand-signed
Poster
Edition of 150

Best known for *Work No. 227* (2000), his Turner Prize-winning installation consisting of lights going on and off in a room, British artist Martin Creed is also a musician. *Love to You*, which *The Guardian* described as 'like something between Steve Reich and The Ramones', is Creed's debut album.

This limited-edition version has been hand-painted by Creed himself at his studio in London. Each of the 150 copies that make up the release is therefore a unique artwork, not only painted but also hand-signed and hand-numbered by the artist. Also included with each copy of the record is a glossy oversized poster of the cover image.
—

PUBLISHER *The Vinyl Factory, UK*
ART DIRECTION *Martin Creed*
DESIGN *Joe Ewart (Society)*
PHOTOGRAPHY *Hugo Glendinning, Martin Creed*
PRODUCTION *The Vinyl Factory*
DATE *2012*

Beatriz Milhazes
Meu Bem

Specifications

Acetate
Art print
Book cloth
Collage
Die cutting
Foil blocking
Foil-surfaced paper
Giclee printing
Hand-bound
Hand-numbered
Hand-signed
Hardback book
Letterpress printing
Millboard
Perspex
Screen printing
Slip case
Edition of 38

The creation of Brazilian artist Beatriz Milhazes, *Meu Bem* was developed over a two-year period and contains a sequence of highly complex pages based on Milhazes's original collages. Every element of the book was hand-produced. Special techniques were devised to give the impression of creases and folds, while a great deal of effort went into producing a book that is clearly part of an edition but also looks unique. Supplied in a yellow Perspex slip case, the book was accompanied by a limited-edition print of one of Milhazes's collages, itself contained in a letterpress-printed folder.

—

PUBLISHER *Ridinghouse (Thomas Dane Gallery), UK*
ART DIRECTION *Beatriz Milhazes*
DESIGN *Book Works Studio*
PRODUCTION *Book Works Studio, K2 Screen*
DATE *2008*

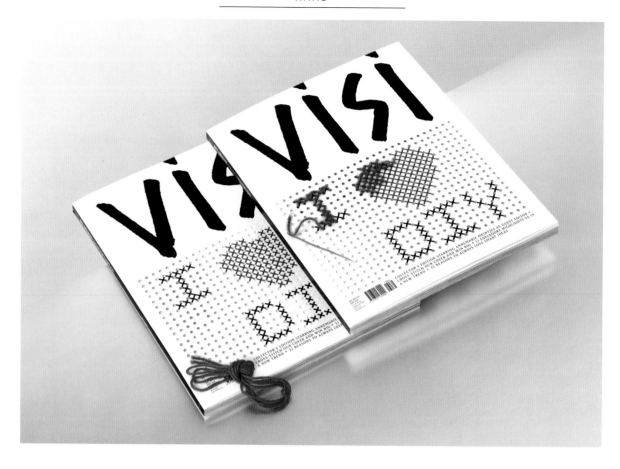

Visi
Issue 64

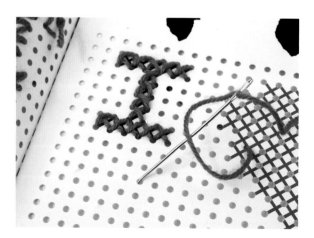

Specifications
6-page gatefold cover
Die cutting
Magazine
Matt Aqueous machine varnish
Red mohair thread
Spot gloss UV varnish

For the cover of its 'DIY Deluxe' edition, South African design, decor and architecture magazine *Visi* wanted something that would make the magazine stand out as a collector's item, as well as communicate its 'alternative DIY' message. After numerous discussions, it was decided that a cross-stitch cover was the ideal solution. The cover was die-cut with a grid of holes large enough for even a novice to have a go, and the magazine was packaged with a length of red wool. With limited space for a pattern, graphic designer Milton Glaser's globally recognized message 'I [heart] NY' became 'I [heart] DIY'.

—

PUBLISHER *New Media Publishing, South Africa*
ART DIRECTION & DESIGN *Anton Pietersen*
PRODUCTION *Paarl Media Paarl, United Varnish and Print Finishing*
DATE *2013*

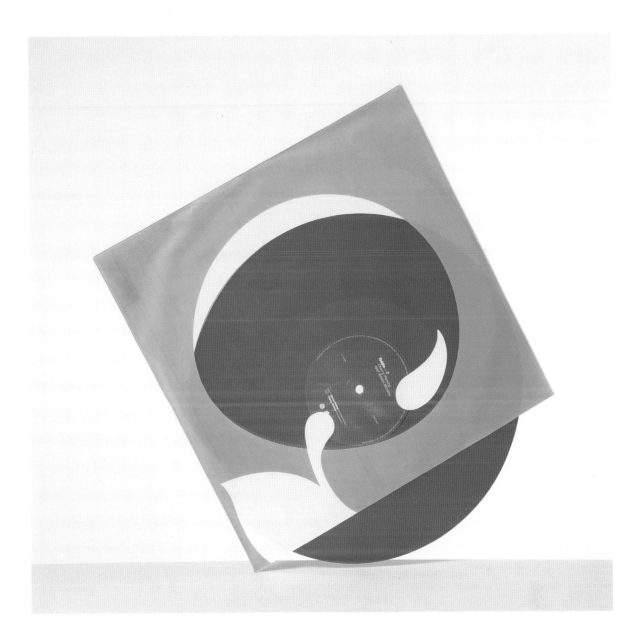

Toddla T
Cherry Picking feat. Roisin Murphy

Specifications
Cherry-red 12" vinyl record
PVC sleeve
Screen printing
Edition of 300

'Cherry Picking', a vinyl-only single by producer Thomas Bell (aka Toddla T), was released for Record Store Day 2011. Limited by time and budget, the designers quickly came up with the idea of using a coloured 12" inside a clear, white and green sleeve to form an illustrated cherry.

—

PUBLISHER *Ninja Tune/Girls Music, UK*
ART DIRECTION *Peter Donohoe, Paul Reardon (Peter and Paul)*
DESIGN *Paul Reardon, Lee Davies*
ILLUSTRATION *Lee Davies*
DATE *2011*

Tejubehan
Drawing from the City

Specifications
Hand-bound
Handmade endpapers
Handmade paper
Hardback book
Screen printing
Section sewing

Tejubehan is a singer and self-taught artist from Ahmedabad in western India, renowned for her rich and detailed drawings. Descended from a community of itinerant musicians, she was encouraged to take up pen and paper by her late husband, Ganesh Jogi, also an artist and musician. *Drawing from the City* is a visual account of her story, a remarkable journey from rural India to life in the city.

The book's designer, Nia Murphy, made the decision to use a large format (36 × 24 cm/14⅛ × 9½ in.) so as not to detract from the intricacy of the artwork. The book was screen-printed on paper made from cotton waste, while the PVC ink that was used was chosen for its ability to retain the depth of Tejubehan's pen-and-ink originals. The printed pages were section-sewn and then hand-bound to the cover, which is made from orange handmade paper.

—

PUBLISHER *Tara Books, India*
ART DIRECTION *Gita Wolf*
DESIGN *Nia Murphy*
ILLUSTRATION *Tejubehan*
PRODUCTION *C. Arumugam, AMM Screens*
DATE *2012*

Dom Thomas
Synthetic Soul

Specifications
2 12" vinyl records
Hand-numbered
Metallic-silver ink
Screen printing
Edition of 100

Producer and remixer Dom
Thomas is also the co-founder of
Brutal Music, part of Manchester-
based Fat City Recordings.
The limited-edition version of
Synthetic Soul, a collection of
remixes, reflects the label's
hands-on ethic, which extends
from the music to the design
and packaging of its releases.
Every copy of *Synthetic Soul*
comes in a screen-printed, hand-
numbered sleeve.

—

PUBLISHER *Brutal Music/Fat City
Recordings, UK*
ART DIRECTION & DESIGN *Dom Thomas*
SCREEN PRINTING *Mission Print*
DATE *2011*

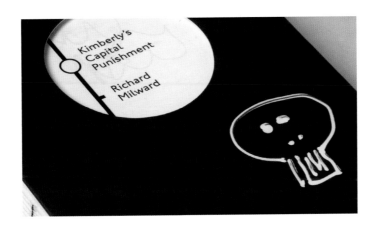

Richard Milward
Kimberly's Capital Punishment

~~~~~~~~~~

Specifications
Die cutting
Hand-drawn artwork
Hand-signed
Section-sewn book block
Slip case
Edition of 300

The special edition of *Kimberly's Capital Punishment*, British writer Richard Milward's third novel, takes the form of a sewn but un-covered book block. Signed by the author, the book block is supplied in a die-cut slip case, which reveals part of the half-title page and features hand-drawn artwork by the author himself. The exposed spine is printed with the words 'Death / Life'.

—

PUBLISHER *Faber and Faber, UK*
DESIGN *Luke Bird (Faber and Faber)*
PRODUCTION *Jack Murphy (Faber and Faber), T. J. International*
DATE *2012*

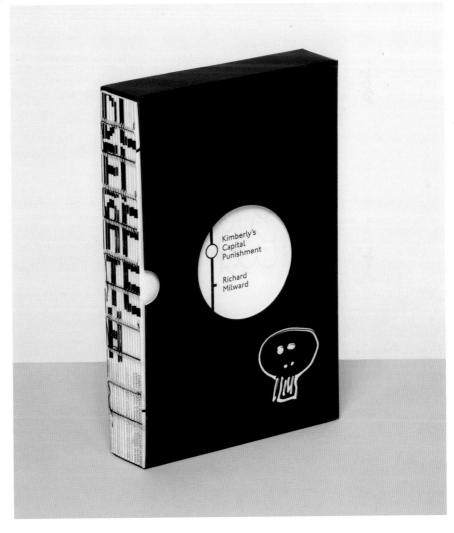

Ice, Sea, Dead People
You Could Be a Model

Specifications
7" vinyl record
Rotating turntable
Sealed-in clear vinyl
Sharpie permanent markers
Edition of 180

These unique 7" picture discs are the result of a collaboration between London-based noise-punk outfit Ice, Sea, Dead People, designer Daniel Eatock and artist Andy Holden. Although this was the first time that Eatock and Holden had worked together on the design of a record, Holden had created a number of record covers before, not only for his own band, The Grubby Mitts, but also for other bands connected with Lost Toys Records. It was, however, their shared interest in repetition and its potential for generation, as well as the role of the hand in the creation of the mass-produced object, that led to their involvement with the project.

The artwork for the picture discs was created during a live performance by Ice, Sea, Dead People at Stanley Picker Gallery at Kingston University in London. As the band began to play 'You Could Be a Model' – the first of the two songs on the double A-sided picture disc – members of the audience were asked to place a pen at the outer edge of a circular piece of paper attached to a turntable rotating at 45 rpm. Their instructions were to move the pen slowly towards the centre of the paper, and to remove the pen only once the song had finished, thereby creating a dense and spiral-shaped graphic representation of the music.

The process was repeated for the second song on the single, 'Ultra Silence', but this time the pen could be moved back and forth between the edge and the centre of the paper, resulting in a more free-form design. The band played the two songs repeatedly until enough pieces of paper had been created for the limited-edition release. Both the A-side and the AA-side pieces of paper were then sealed inside clear 7" vinyl, on to which the single's two tracks were later cut. The records were released commercially through Lost Toys Records, with each record representing a unique document of the live event – the translation of a song into a line. As far as it is known, this is the first time that every record in a picture-disc series has featured unique artwork.

—

PUBLISHER *Lost Toys Records, UK*
ART DIRECTION & DESIGN
Daniel Eatock, Andy Holden
DATE *2012*

MaMa
Project Bootleg feat. Apparat, Deadmau5, Die Antwood, Gold Panda, The Roots

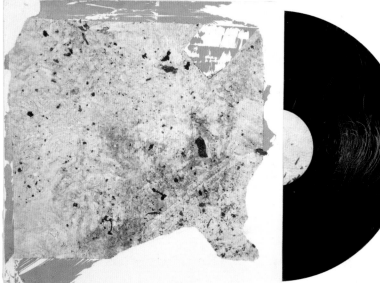

Specifications
12" vinyl records
Brown tape
Feet
White cardboard

Project Bootleg is the brainchild of German creative duo Maximilian Hoch and Manuel Urbanke, aka MaMa. Prompted by the fact that scratches on records are seen as something bad, the duo set out to make music out of these scratches.

The project began life as uncut 12" records. These 'empty' pieces of vinyl were then taped to the floor at various music concerts, including shows by Deadmau5 and Gold Panda. As the crowds danced and jumped around, the records became scratched; when the records were played, these scratches produced sounds.

German experimental musician Daniel Freitag was recruited to transform the sounds into a more consumable form of music. The 'recordings' were digitized and then mixed in the studio to create a series of downloadable tracks.

—

PUBLISHER *MaMa, Germany*
ART DIRECTION & DESIGN
Maximilian Hoch, Manuel Urbanke
DATE *2012–13*

Cryptik
Eastern Philosophy

Specifications

10 screen prints
Hand-antiqued paper
Hand-numbered
Hand painting
Hand-signed
Hardback book
Laser-etched dividers
Linen sack
Redwood box
Screen printing
Unique copper Buddha
Edition of 12

Cryptik is the enigmatic artist behind the Cryptik Movement, which, according to its website, is 'a public art campaign dedicated to helping humanity evolve towards greater awareness and understanding through the use of compelling, iconic imagery'. *Eastern Philosophy* is a collection of Cryptik's street art, including his distinctive images of the Buddha, Gandhi and the Hindu deity Ganesha, as captured by various artists and photographers.

This deluxe artist's edition comes in a redwood box, the exterior of which has been hand-painted by Cryptik himself. Lined with a specially designed paper, the box has been made to look like an antique, complete with rusty hinges. Included in the box is a screen-printed linen sack in which to store the book, a unique screen-printed copper Buddha and ten two-colour screen prints of Cryptik's work.

—

PUBLISHER *ZERO+ Publishing, USA*
ART DIRECTION *Kirk Pedersen*
DESIGN *Kirk Pedersen, Cryptik*
ARTWORK *Cryptik*
PRODUCTION *Cryptik*
DATE *2012*

The Vatican Secret Archives
Collector's Edition

The Vatican Secret Archives is the first book to offer a behind-the-scenes look at one of the most extraordinary archives in the world. Estimated to consist of some 85 kilometres (53 miles) of shelving, and containing documents that date back to the eighth century, the Archivio Segreto Vaticano has served the Holy See for more than 400 years.

Of the two limited editions of *Archives* produced by its publisher, VdH Books of Belgium, the collector's is by far the most exclusive. The first three copies of the book, which is limited to an edition of thirty-three (the age at which Christ was crucified), were given to the Pope, the Vatican Library and the archives themselves. The remaining thirty copies were put on general sale.

The aim was to produce something truly unique. Each copy is printed individually, on demand, in one of four languages (Italian, English, French or Dutch), as chosen by the buyer. It is then moved to the studios of the archives, where it is hand-bound using centuries-old techniques. Finally, each copy is certified as authentic by the prefect of the archives.

—

PUBLISHER *VdH Books, Belgium*
ART DIRECTION *Paul Van den Heuvel*
DESIGN *Kevin Vanden Neucker (New Goff, Graphius Group)*
PHOTOGRAPHY *Andrea Marini, Philippe Debeerst, Enrico Ottaviani*
PRODUCTION *New Goff*
DATE *2009*

Specifications
Alum-tawed goat leather
Gold foil
Hand-bound
Hand-numbered
Hardback book
Sewed-on ribbon
Sheep parchment
Edition of 33

Madlib
Madlib Medicine Show #11: Low Budget High Fi Music

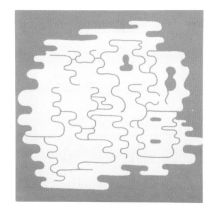

Specifications
3 12" vinyl records
Cannabis smoke
Hennessy cognac
Paint
Screen printing

'Madlib Medicine Show' was a series of hip-hop and remix albums released by American musician, DJ and producer Otis Jackson Jr, aka Madlib, on his own label. Originally intended to be a twelve-album series lasting a year, the project took two years to complete and ended up consisting of thirteen different releases. The triple-vinyl limited edition of release no. 11 features a series of unique screen-printed sleeves made with paint infused with Hennessy and cannabis smoke. According to designer Jeff Jank, the idea to 'customize' the paint in this way came from the sleeves' printers, Hit+Run of Los Angeles – because, he explains, 'they work best with what they have sitting around the studio'.
—

PUBLISHER *Madlib Invazion, USA*
ART DIRECTION & DESIGN *Jeff Jank*
ILLUSTRATION *Gustavo Eandi, Isabel Samaras*
PRODUCTION *Hit+Run*
DATE *2012*

Samuel Taylor Coleridge
The Rime of the Ancient Mariner

Specifications

22-carat gold blocked on spine
Foil blocking in 4 metallic foils
Gilded top edge
Hand-bound
Hand-printed engraving
Hardback book
Letterpress-printed endpapers
Signed and numbered
Solander box
Text borders printed in gold ink
Tipped-in illustrations
Vellum spine
Edition of 1,000

This special edition of Samuel Taylor Coleridge's lengthy narrative poem was inspired by the deluxe illustrated editions of classic works of literature produced in the early years of the twentieth century. Like many of those books, it has been quarter-bound in vellum, an expensive yet superior book-binding material. The elaborate blocking design, the tipped-in illustrations and the hand-printed frontispiece are all special features intended to enhance the reader's experience.

One of the great poems of Romanticism, 'The Rime of the Ancient Mariner' was first published in 1798. This edition follows the revised version of 1817, and includes three other poems by Coleridge: 'Christabel', 'Kubla Khan' and 'The Pains of Sleep'.

—

PUBLISHER *The Folio Society, UK*
ART DIRECTION *Joe Whitlock Blundell*
ILLUSTRATION *Harry Brockway*
CALLIGRAPHY *Stephen Raw*
TYPOGRAPHY *Joe Whitlock Blundell*
PRODUCTION *Martins the Printers, Napier Jones, I. M. Imprimit, The Logan Press, The Fine Book Bindery*
DATE *2010*

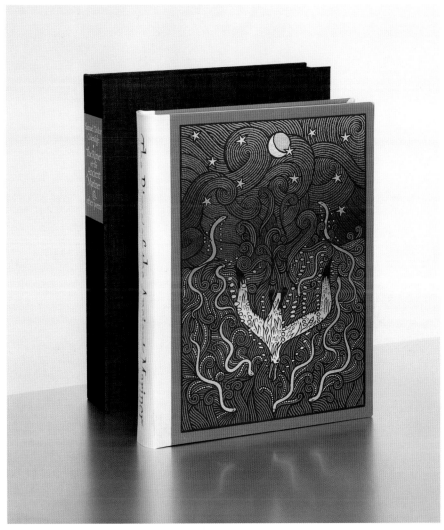

Kid Acne
Council Pop, 10th Anniversary Edition

~~~~~~~~~~~~

Specifications
3 12" vinyl records
Embossing
Hand finishing
Hand-numbered
Hand-signed
Risograph printing
Screen printing
Edition of 33

Council Pop, the second album by Sheffield-based artist and hip-hop musician Kid Acne, was originally released in 2003. Following the discovery in his cellar of some forgotten copies of the album, Kid Acne decided to mark the tenth anniversary of its release by giving these remaining copies a makeover and putting them out as a limited edition.

Beginning with the outer sleeve, Kid Acne added screen prints to both the front and the back. He then screen-printed the inner sleeve, and added a Risograph-printed insert. Also included is an LP of instrumentals and a 12" of the single from the album, 'Radio Music', which has been hand-finished with a marker pen. Each copy of the limited edition has been signed and numbered by Kid Acne.

—

PUBLISHER *Kid Acne/Invisible Spies, UK*
ART DIRECTION & DESIGN *Kid Acne*
PHOTOGRAPHY *Ian Newcomb*
ILLUSTRATION *Kid Acne*
SCREEN PRINTING *Kid Acne*
DATE *2013*

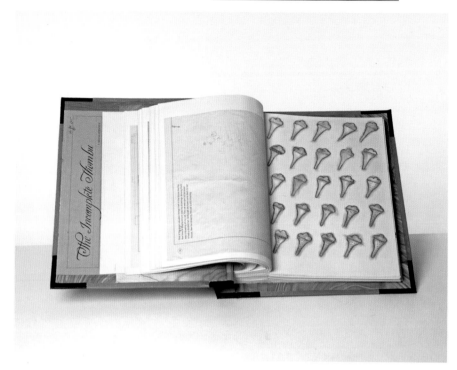

Specifications
Dry pastel
Embossing
Foil stamping
Hardback book
Hand-bound
Handmade board
Handmade paper
Hand marbling
Original artwork
Screen printing
Edition of 25

T. Shanaathanan
The Incomplete Thombu

In *The Incomplete Thombu*, Sri Lankan artist T. Shanaathanan addresses the subject of Tamil displacement during the Sri Lankan Civil War (1983–2009). Through a series of drawings, each made in response to personal and official records of Tamil-owned properties as they were prior to the displacements, Shanaathanan highlights the oft-neglected plight of those affected. The large size of this special edition (30.5 × 22 cm/12 × 8⅝ in.) is intended to recall the large-format land-registry files, or 'thombu', used in Sri Lanka.

Based around the book block printed for the standard edition, the special edition has been hand-bound using the binding method currently employed by the technical branch of the Sri Lanka Department of National Archives. Accompanying the book is an original artwork by Shanaathanan: a screen print with added dry pastel on handmade acid-free paper. The colophon was printed on a Golding Jobber printing press from the early 1900s, one of the few letterpress machines of its kind still in existence – and still in use in Sri Lanka. At either end of the book are endpapers that have been marbled by hand.

—

PUBLISHER *Raking Leaves, Sri Lanka*
ART DIRECTION *Sharmini Pereira*
DESIGN *Deshan Tennekoon, Asvajit Boyle*
PRODUCTION *Muwini Silva and Padmini Jayalath (endpapers), Nimal Joseph (hand-binding), Gunawardena Block Makers, Amila Karunadhara (letterpress printing), Gunaratne Offset*
DATE *2011*

Ssaliva
RZA & Sync Thrills

Specifications
Gold 10" vinyl record (*RZA*)
Letterpress printing
Metal lines
Metal type
Pink 10" vinyl record
(*Sync Thrills*)
Screen printing
Wooden type

Co-founded in 2010 by graphic designer Dimitri Runkkari, Vlek is an independent Belgian record label specializing in electronic music. Notably, all of its releases are issued on vinyl, as well as digitally, with every sleeve designed and printed by Runkkari himself. Each of the label's releases is limited to a maximum of 500 copies.

RZA and *Sync Thrills* are the first two records in a trilogy of EPs by Belgian producer François Boulanger, aka Ssaliva. The sleeves for both EPs feature highly linear designs – partly as a result of Runkkari finding a box of metal lines used in letterpress.

In the case of *RZA*, Runkkari wanted to find a way of writing the artist's name using such lines, in the style of the logo for the 1968 Mexico Olympics. Samples of the lines were manipulated in Photoshop to form the word 'Ssaliva'. The resulting image was then screen-printed.

For *Sync Thrills*, Runkkari took a different approach. After recording the word 'Ssaliva', he made a screenshot of the soundwave it made. Then, using a printout of the soundwave as a template, he carefully placed the found metal lines on the bed of a printing press – thus recreating the shape of the soundwave – and printed the image.
—

PUBLISHER *Vlek, Belgium*
ART DIRECTION & DESIGN
Dimitri Runkkari
PRINTING *Dimitri Runkkari*
DATE *2012*

STEFAN

SAGMEISTER

INTERVIEW : MATTHEW LEE

PHOTOGRAPH : EMILIANO GRANADO

STEFAN SAGMEISTER is an Austrian graphic designer and typographer who has lived and worked in New York since 1993. His clients have included the Rolling Stones, Lou Reed and David Byrne. Every seven years he takes a year off from commercial work; he spent his most recent sabbatical in Bali, the home of Barbadian artist Ashley Bickerton. His design studio, Sagmeister & Walsh, which he set up with designer Jessica Walsh, was commissioned to produce a collector's edition of Bickerton's monograph (2011; see page 184).

How did your collaboration with Ashley Bickerton come about?

Other Criteria [an arts-based publishing company founded by Damien Hirst] had approached me before I went on my sabbatical to Bali. I knew and liked Ashley's work, was aware that he lived in Bali, and thought this would be a good opportunity to get to know him and talk in depth about his work. I only started the design work proper when I returned from Bali, so I'd say that, overall, it was an ideal situation: Ashley and I became friends in Bali, and I got to know his work really well, all before we designed a single page.

Did any of your previous projects inform the Ashley Bickerton limited edition, or was your work purely a response to Ashley's art?

Very much the latter. The idea for the slip case became clear right away. I had commissioned a lot of work in Bali with incredible craftspeople, and Ashley had always used very elaborate frames in his work.

What was working with Ashley like?

He was a fantastic client. Throughout the project he encouraged us to take liberties, and I had become very fond of his writing. We only had one argument during the entire production process. I had pushed for a smaller publication than the big book we made, which would have sold at a cheaper price.

Did you have creative freedom on this project?

We wanted to represent Ashley's work as well as we could in book form. We were in agreement that this did not mean art uncropped on white backgrounds, because we all felt that the majority of art books are boring. Ashley encouraged us to look at his work and interpret it – its surroundings, its process, its thinking.

The regular edition of the book features a number of specialist production techniques, such as silver and black paper edging, but the limited edition pushes this concept much further. How did you carve the pattern on the paper edging?

In Bali I had commissioned numerous projects with various wood-carvers, and while visiting one craftsman it became clear that a book is nothing more than a wooden block and, as such, could be carved. We clamped down an old book and asked him to make a test carving, and it worked extremely well. The regular and limited editions are very similar. The difference is in the fore-edge, the added print and the slip case. We designed them at the same time, so it was easy to coordinate the process.

You worked with German designer Philipp Hubert on custom-designed typography. How did the 'orchid' type style develop?

Philipp did much more than just design the custom type. He designed much of the book and did a lot of the heavy lifting. The type was inspired by mother-of-pearl inlays, also seen in Ashley's frames.

Was your choice of materials for the slip case [mother-of-pearl, Balinese wood, gold and brass coins] informed by your experience of living in Indonesia?

Completely. It's a through-and-through craft-oriented society. And Ashley was very fond of it, too.

How labour-intensive was the production process?

The carving for the fifty books took about four months. We ended up using Ashley's frame-carver for the slip case, as the carvers I've worked with do not have clean enough workspaces to deal with something like a book, which needed to be handled very carefully.

Did you learn anything new about your own craft, working with Balinese craftspeople?

Just that there is an incredible satisfaction in the experience of making something by hand and seeing it completed.

'In Bali I had commissioned numerous projects with various wood-carvers, and while visiting one craftsman it became clear that a book is nothing more than a wooden block and, as such, could be carved.'

You're known for your exploration of the nature of happiness. Did Bali make you happy?

I kept a 'level of well-being' score throughout this period, so I can tell you exactly. During my time in Bali, while I was meditating, my score was 6.7 out of 10. It was much lower in the months before, a guesstimated 5 out of 10.

The cost of the special edition [£2,500] is many times greater than the cost of the normal edition. Is this price tag a reflection of its quality or of its scarcity?

It's a reflection of both things.

Did you feel any pressure having to create something with such a high price tag?

Well, it's a different market. The limited edition is geared towards collectors. Once you've bought an original Ashley Bickerton, the £2,500 book that contains another original might not seem like that much money.

Is there ever an issue with motivation when you're working on something like this, which will be viewed by an extremely small audience, as opposed to a project for the likes of the Rolling Stones, which will be seen by millions?

No, but I do prefer good projects with very large audiences. They are also much harder to do.

For whose art do you think people buy the book, Ashley Bickerton's or Stefan Sagmeister's?

They are buying Ashley Bickerton's art, as interpreted for the book by Stefan Sagmeister.

Is our relationship with printed objects changing as our media landscape becomes increasingly digital?

Yes, of course. It seems there is much more interest in the special, scarce, tactile object. I see a growing interest in highly crafted objects.

How do you select the clients with whom you work?

We love kind clients with interesting projects, proper deadlines – and generous budgets.

Stefan Sagmeister was photographed at the Lehmann Maupin Gallery, 201 Chrystie Street, New York, USA

Ashley Bickerton
Monograph

Specifications
Art print
Balinese wood
Brass coins
Die cutting
Hand carving
Hand-cut paper edges
Hand-numbered
Hand-signed
Hardback book
Mother-of-pearl
Poster
Pressed orchids
Recycled teak
Slip case
Edition of 50

Born in Barbados, Ashley Bickerton is a contemporary artist currently living on the island of Bali. Published in both standard and limited editions, this monograph – the first on the artist – offers a comprehensive visual survey of Bickerton's career. Interwoven with the artist's own commentary are an essay by fellow artist Jake Chapman and an interview with the critic, curator and historian Hans-Ulrich Obrist presented in the form of a comic strip. The limited edition, which comes in a wooden slip case carved in Bali, features hand-carving on the exposed edges of the book block, a signed print of Bickerton's work and pressed orchids.

—

PUBLISHER *Other Criteria, UK*
ART DIRECTION *Stefan Sagmeister (Sagmeister & Walsh)*
DESIGN & TYPOGRAPHY *Philipp Hubert*
GRAPHIC ARTIST *Ignacio Noé*
DATE *2011*

Giant Drag
Shredding Leeds

Specifications
12" vinyl record
Embossing powder
Fabric paint
Hairspray
Hand-mixed glitter
Hand stamping
Spray paint
Stained glass
Stencil
Unique artefact

Shredding Leeds, a live album recorded in England in 2006 by American indie rock band Giant Drag, was released in three vinyl editions, as well as digitally. The packaging for 'Version Three', aka 'Super Deluxe, Grab Bag Reminiscent, Even More Limited, Fullest Psycho Edition', is almost entirely handmade, from the hand-stamped track listing to the glitter-decorated outer sleeve. Each copy is hand-finished by the band's lead singer, Annie Hardy, while the added extras, such as handmade guitar knobs, can vary from copy to copy. Common to each one is a membership card for the Giant Drag fan club.
—

PUBLISHER *Full Psycho Records, USA*
ART DIRECTION *Annie Hardy*
DESIGN *Annie Hardy, Colin MacCubbin, Monica Barcicki, 'Stevue' Nick Liberatore, Ann Jones*
PHOTOGRAPHY *Tony Steinberg*
ILLUSTRATION *Vanessa Von Valkenberg*
PRODUCTION *Monica Barcicki*
DATE *2013*

This limited edition of *WIXIW*, the sixth studio album by American alternative rock trio Liars, comprises a vinyl copy of the original album inside a specially made sleeve. The intention behind the limited-edition sleeve was to create something that felt physically different from the original cover. This was achieved by dipping the sleeve, which by this time had already been screen-printed with the Liars' 'L' logo, into wax – a process performed by Liars themselves. The album's title was then imprinted into the wax while it was still warm. Finally, each of the 300 copies of the sleeve was numbered by hand.

—

PUBLISHER *Mute, UK*
ART DIRECTION & DESIGN *John Wiese*
WAX-DIPPING *Liars*
PRODUCTION *Mute*
DATE *2012*

Liars
WIXIW

Specifications
12" vinyl record
Black liquid dye
Hand-numbered
Hand wax-dipping
Screen printing
Soy-based candle wax
Uncoated board
Edition of 300

Kottie Paloma
XOXO: Poster Edition

Specifications
Acrylic paint
Archival box
Fluorescent paint
Hand-numbered
Hand-signed
Hand stamping
Original artwork
Paperback book
Poster print
Spray paint
Stencil
Edition of 50

Kottie Paloma is an American-born artist based in Berlin. According to his website, his art is concerned with 'the ridiculousness of life', while much of the text in his work is taken from overheard conversations, the lyrics to his favourite songs and memories of past experiences.

The original idea behind *XOXO*, a survey of Paloma's work from the period 2010 to 2012, was to produce an edition of 1,000 copies. However, after the initial work on the book had been completed, Paloma met with the book's German publisher, PogoBooks, to discuss other ways in which it could be presented. The decision was made to produce something unique, with

a signed copy of the book and a signed limited-edition poster of Paloma's work.

When it was suggested to Paloma that the book and poster could be packaged in a plain archival box, he offered to provide a series of original artworks for the front of the boxes. Within a fortnight, he had produced fifty-two original paintings (fifty for the boxes and two artist's proofs). Copies of the book can now be found in the collections of Stanford and Harvard universities in the United States.

—

PUBLISHER *PogoBooks Verlag, Germany*
ART DIRECTION *Claudio Pfeifer*
ART *Kottie Paloma*
DATE *2012*

Der Greif
Issue 6

Specifications
Brass rubbing
Hand-numbered
Hand-signed
Magazine
Personalized dedication
Recycled paper
Edition of 2,000

Der Greif is a German
photography and literary
magazine, the main aim of which
is to present the work of a range
of different artists within a single
issue. Photographers and writers
are invited to submit their work
via the magazine's website.
The designers then 'curate' the
selected photographs and texts to
create the magazine's content.

Produced in a large format
(35 × 25 cm/13¾ × 9⅞ in.), the
magazine is limited to a print run
of 2,000 copies per issue, each
of which is numbered by hand.
This collector's edition of issue
6 includes a personalized, brass-
rubbed dedication signed by
the publishers.

—

PUBLISHERS *Simon Karlstetter, Leon
Kirchlechner, Matthias Lohscheidt*
DESIGN *Leon Kirchlechner, Simon Karlstetter*
COVER PHOTOGRAPH *Simon Karlstetter*
DATE *2012*

Massive Attack
Atlas Air

Specifications

12" vinyl record
Diamond dust
Hand-signed
Hand stamping
Laser etching
Screen printing
White board
Yellow fluorescent ink
Edition of 1,000

Released in aid of War Child, this limited-edition EP is taken from *Heligoland*, the fourth album by Bristol-based musical collective Massive Attack. The screen-printed artwork is an adaptation of *Minstrels*, a painting by Massive Attack's Robert Del Naja, produced in his studio at the time of the album's recording. The screen print has been treated with diamond dust, a reflection of Del Naja's interest in the colonial history of the band's home city and the wealth that it generated. Similar themes are explored on the EP itself.

—

PUBLISHER *The Vinyl Factory, UK*
ART DIRECTION *Robert Del Naja, Tom Hingston Studio*
DESIGN *Tom Hingston Studio*
ARTWORK *Robert Del Naja*
PRODUCTION *The Vinyl Factory, K2 Screen*
DATE *2010*

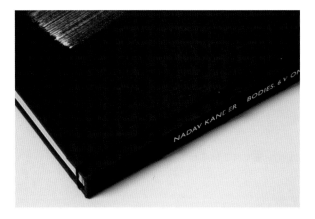

Nadav Kander
Bodies. 6 Women, 1 Man

Specifications
2 photographic prints
Foil stamping
Hardback book
Handmade box
Hand painting
Japanese stab binding
Vellum divider pages
White paint
Edition of 100

Bodies. 6 Women, 1 Man is a striking collection of nude portraits by London-based Israeli photographer Nadav Kander. 'These pictures are the latest, and perhaps strongest, distillation of the themes that continue to fascinate and nourish me', he explains. 'My subject matter is varied but the essence is the same ... I work with the human conditions that link us all ... What it is to be alone in the world. What it is to be human.' This collector's edition features a unique hand-painted cover by Kander himself. The white paint echoes the hand-applied paint and dust that was used to cover all the bodies photographed for the book.

—

PUBLISHER *Hatje Cantz Verlag, Germany*
ART DIRECTION *Nadine Schmidt, Markus Hartmann, Tappin Gofton, Nadav Kander*
DESIGN *Tappin Gofton*
PHOTOGRAPHY *Nadav Kander*
PRODUCTION *Druckerei Grammlich*
DATE *2013*

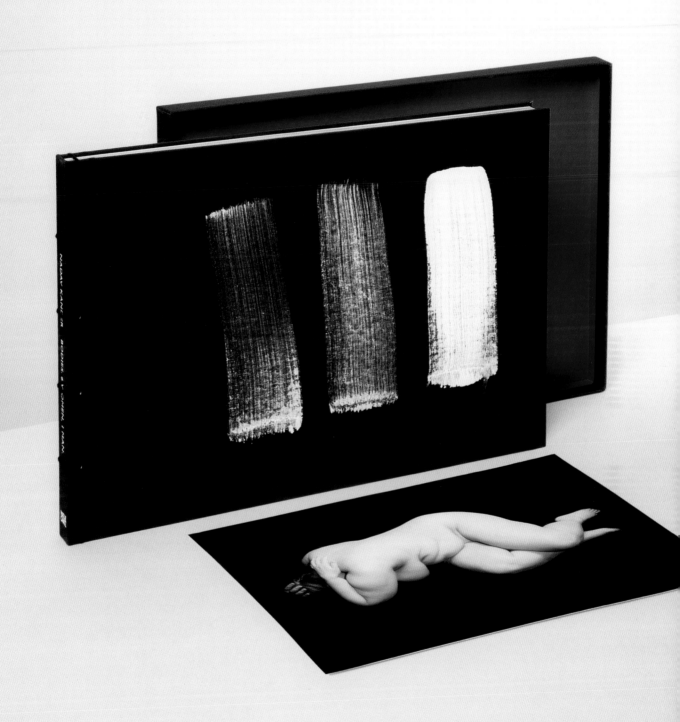

Yoko Ogawa
Revenge

Specifications
Handmade chemise
Hand-signed
Hardback book
Japanese kimono silk
Edition of 100

According to Simon Rhodes, production manager at Harvill Secker, the issue of how to treat the special edition of *Revenge* by Japanese writer Yoko Ogawa was quickly resolved. 'From the beginning', he explains, '[Publishing Director] Liz Foley and I had a very clear idea of what we wanted to do with the book: bind it in Japanese silk.'

The main challenge was working out how best to do this. Several binding methods were explored, but it was decided that the chemise was the best option because it interfered the least with the feel and structure of the silk. Of critical importance to the success of the project was bookbinder Midori Kunikata-Cockram and her knowledge of

the materials and great skill in working with them.

The quality and design of the silk were also crucial. After a period of research, and with the help of an expert on kimonos and their manufacture, Kunikata-Cockram bought two bolts of kimono silk and one actual kimono, which provided three different patterns. She then made each chemise by hand, ensuring that no two are the same. Finally, the books were signed by the author and wrapped in shoji and chiyogami handmade paper.

—

PUBLISHER *Harvill Secker, UK*
ART DIRECTION *Simon Rhodes, Midori Kunikata-Cockram (Jade Bookbinding Studio)*
PRODUCTION *Midori Kunikata-Cockram (chemises), GGP Media GmbH (books)*
DATE *2013*

Coppice
Vinculum

Specifications
12 CDs
Brass
Copper mesh
Cork
Embroidery
Galvanized steel
Glass
Handmade pouch
Magnets
Onion
Recycled fabric
Redwood
Rubber
Screen printing
Specimen box
Twine
Edition of 5

Coppice is an experimental music duo composed of Chicago-based Noé Cuéllar and Joseph Kramer. Among the duo's numerous creations are original compositions, installations and music-related sculpture. *Vinculum* is a growing archive of 'sonic artefacts'. Started in 2010, it consists of a series of recorded and manipulated sounds on single-track CDs.

The 'Vinculum Specimen Edition' box set comprises a handmade box (which also doubles as a musical instrument) containing twelve *Vinculum* CDs. The box set is available as part of a number of different packages, including this 'Collector's Level' package. Among the extra items included are three bonus CDs in a handmade, pyramid-shaped box, unreleased recordings in a handmade pouch – and an onion.

—

PUBLISHER *Coppice, USA*
ART DIRECTION *Coppice*
DESIGN *Coppice, Andrew Furse, Jenny Vallier*
PRODUCTION *Andrew Furse, Jenny Vallier*
DATE *2010*

~~~~~~~~~~~~~~~~~~

Oscar Tuazon
I Can't See

Specifications
Cement
Hand-signed certificate
Oak frame
Paper
Edition of 45 + 5 APs

For this special edition of *I Can't See*, a monograph on the work of American contemporary artist Oscar Tuazon, the artist himself has transformed more than forty copies of the book into a series of unique 'papercrete' objects. Each of these objects consists of a single copy of *I Can't See* that has been shredded, mixed with water and cement, and reformed to resemble the original publication. Housed in an oak frame, the result, according to the publishers, is 'an unreadable book, a book as a material thing, words turned to stone'.

—

PUBLISHER *DoPe Press, USA*
PRODUCTION *Oscar Tuazon*
DATE *2011*

Specifications
Acrylic paint
CD
Glitter
Hand-numbered
Hand-signed
Spray paint
Stencils

Formed in 2009, Icona Pop is a Swedish dance music duo. The collector's edition of *Iconic EP* is a unique, handmade version of the band's 2012 breakthrough release personally designed and painted by bandmates Aino Jawo and Caroline Hjelt. Each CD is signed and numbered in an edition of fewer than 1,000.

To create the artwork, blank CD wallets were arranged in such a way as to form large 'canvases' for the band to work on. Using a variety of tools and materials, Jawo and Hjelt then created five highly colourful designs. As a piece of the larger canvases, each CD is distinct from every other in the series.

—

PUBLISHER *Warner Music, USA*
ART DIRECTION & DESIGN
Aino Jawo, Caroline Hjelt
PRODUCTION *Aino Jawo, Caroline Hjelt*
DATE *2013*

Icona Pop
Iconic EP

Justin Velor
2013

Specifications
2 12" vinyl records
Box sleeve
Hand stamping
Metallic-silver ink
Screen printing
Thai hand-marbled paper
Edition of 100

Justin Velor is an alias of Dom Thomas, producer, remixer and record-label boss (see page 166). Described by Thomas as 'a musical Frankenstein's monster', *2013* is the first album to be released under the Velor name. The hand-marbled sleeves are intended to reflect the diverse nature of the album's content.

—

PUBLISHER *Brutal Music/Fat City Recordings, UK*
ART DIRECTION & DESIGN *Dom Thomas*
PRODUCTION *Hastings Box Company, Mission Print*
DATE *2013*

Plinth
Collected Machine Music

Specifications
150-year-old engravings
Brass nuts and bolts
CD
Clock hands
Collage
Hand printing
Hand-punched song strip
Hand-signed
Music box
Stained oak
Victorian calling cards
Edition of 70

This special edition of *Collected Machine Music* by British musician Michael Tanner, aka Plinth, takes the form of a highly decorated music box fashioned from a chocolate box. The album itself was created from the various sounds made by some Victorian parlour-music machines, a French carillon and an old calliope (a musical instrument that produces sound by forcing steam or compressed air through large whistles).

Each of the edition's seventy boxes is unique, having been hand-finished with original engravings, Victorian calling cards, clock hands and other period ephemera. Included in each box is a signed, numbered and hand-annotated song strip from Tanner. Each song strip carries a tune that is unique to that box; composed by Tanner on a harp, the song was subsequently transcribed to the song strip by hand, one hole-punch at a time.

—

PUBLISHER *Time Released Sound, USA*
ART DIRECTION & DESIGN *Colin Herrick*
DATE *2012*

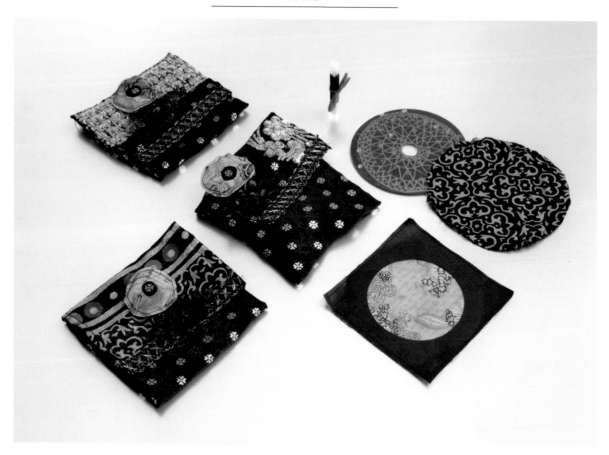

Greenpot Bluepot
Ascend at the Dead End

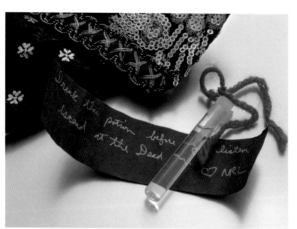

Specifications
Book pages
Brooch
CD
Cotton
Glass vial
Hand-drawn artwork
Hand sewing
Hand-written scroll
Netting
Silk pouch
Silk veil

The packaging for the limited edition of *Ascend at the Dead End* by Natalie LeBrecht, aka Greenpot Bluepot, is based on LeBrecht's own system of divination. Made by LeBrecht herself, it includes a fragrant silk pouch for the CD, a 'relic infusion' in a glass vial, and a brooch made from silk, netting, cotton and pages taken from a Philip K. Dick novel.

—

PUBLISHER *Greenpot Bluepot, USA*
ART DIRECTION & DESIGN
Natalie LeBrecht
DATE *2012*

Specifications

22-carat gold blocked on spine
Foil blocking in 4 metallic foils
Gilded top edge
Hand-bound
Hand-printed engraving
Hardback book
Letterpress-printed endpapers
Signed and numbered
Solander box
Text borders printed in gold ink
Tipped-in illustrations
Vellum spine
Edition of 1,000

Rudyard Kipling's *Just So Stories* was first published in 1902, at a time when book illustration was thriving. However, although some of Kipling's other books appeared as lavishly illustrated editions, *Just So Stories* was never treated in this way. This limited edition of The Folio Society's *Stories* goes some way towards redressing the balance, featuring fourteen illustrations by Thai artist Niroot Puttapipat.

The book itself has been quarter-bound in vellum. The spine has been blocked in 22-carat gold, while four different metallic foils have been used for the front cover. Five printing houses were involved in the book's production, each with expertise in different media and techniques. Each book also features a hand-printed etching by Puttapipat. Hand-numbered and signed by the artist, it has been tipped in by hand and set within a decorative gold border.

—

PUBLISHER *The Folio Society, UK*
ART DIRECTION & DESIGN
Joe Whitlock Blundell
ILLUSTRATION *Niroot Puttapipat*
CALLIGRAPHY *Stephen Raw*
ETCHING *Bacon & Bacon*
PRODUCTION *Martins the Printers, Dot Gradations, R. B. Print, Full Spectrum Print Media, The Logan Press, The Fine Book Bindery, G. Ryder & Co.*
DATE *2012*

Rudyard Kipling
Just So Stories

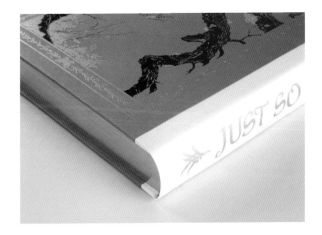

Haruki Murakami
1Q84

Specifications
3 paperback books
Certificate of authenticity
Coloured thread
Hand-bound
Hand-signed
Letterpress printing
Perspex slip case
Edition of 111

This limited edition of Haruki Murakami's novel *1Q84* was inspired by the tradition of the artist's book. Imagining the three volumes as blank canvases, the project's creative team wanted to find a way to express the essence of the story visually. The resulting geometric shapes are intended to suggest the two moons that characterize the world known as '1Q84' and the novel's interweaving realities.

The making of the books was predominantly manual, from the hand-bound, exposed-spine book blocks to the letterpress-printed covers. Bespoke inks were created to ensure a consistency of colour between the binding thread, the letterpress and the hand-finished paper edges. Finally, the slip-cased books were hand-stitched into a cloth parcel.

—

PUBLISHER *Harvill Secker, UK*
ART DIRECTION *Kristen Harrison
(The Curved House), Simon Rhodes*
DESIGN *Stefanie Posavec*
LETTERPRESS *Justin Knopp (Typoretum)*
PRODUCTION *Graphicom*
DATE *2011*

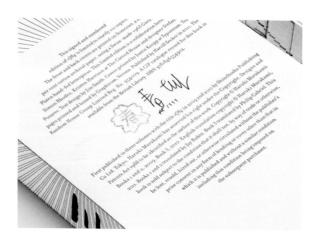

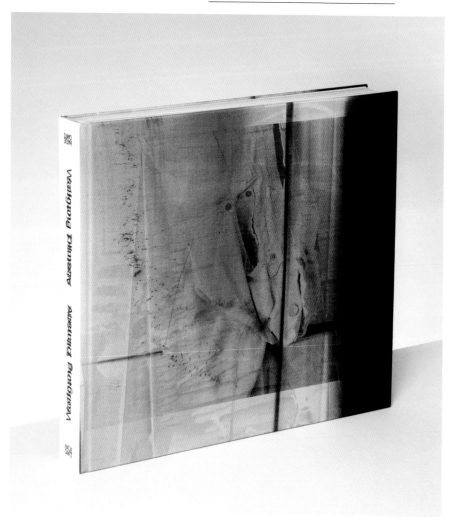

Specifications
Book cloth
Hardback book
Kraft paper
Printer's registration sheets
Edition of 176

Abstract Pictures is a collection of some of the more abstract works by German fine-art photographer Wolfgang Tillmans. This collector's edition of the book has been assembled by hand from the registration sheets produced during the printing of the standard edition. Significantly, however, these sheets have been overprinted with a random selection of abstract forms, which Tillmans created himself by adding ink to the rollers of the printing press, a Heidelberg Speedmaster XL 162. Composed of doubled, smudged and layered images, the result is a fascinating, one-of-a-kind publication, signed and numbered by the artist.
—

PUBLISHER *Hatje Cantz Verlag, Germany*
ART DIRECTION & DESIGN
Wolfgang Tillmans
PHOTOGRAPHY *Wolfgang Tillmans*
PRODUCTION *Markus Hartmann,
Dr. Cantz'sche Druckerei*
DATE *2011*

Wolfgang Tillmans
Abstract Pictures

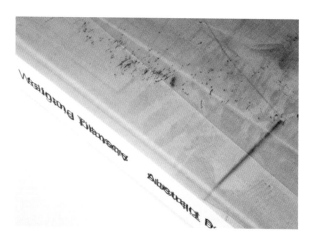

Mark E
Crossing Paths/R-Type

Specifications
12" vinyl record
Acrylic paint
Cardboard
Edition of 50

Crossing Paths/R-Type is
Birmingham-based DJ and
producer Mark E's first release
for Bokhari Records. To celebrate
Record Store Day 2013, the record
label commissioned British artist
Ian Stevenson to produce fifty
different hand-painted sleeves
for the EP. As fans of Ian's work,
the label felt that a record sleeve
would be the perfect medium for
his particular brand of humour.
Acrylic paint allowed Stevenson
to paint directly on to the sleeves.
—

PUBLISHER *Bokhari Records, UK*
COVER ART *Ian Stevenson*
DATE *2013*

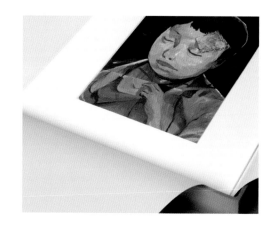

Andrew Hem
Dreams Towards Reality

Specifications
5 original artworks
Bamboo box
Clamshell box
Cloth portfolio
Food jars
Hand-numbered
Hand painting
Hand-signed
Hardback book
Matchboxes
Stencil
Edition of 9

For this 'bamboo box' limited edition of *Dreams Towards Reality*, a survey of the work of Andrew Hem, the Los Angeles-based artist originally wanted to laser-etch the surfaces of the handmade box. After a failed test run, it became clear to Hem that he should paint a unique character on the lid of each box instead. The other items of original artwork supplied with the box include nine mini portraits on matchboxes, a painting on paper and a painted sculpture made from two food jars.

—

PUBLISHER *ZERO+ Publishing, USA*
ART DIRECTION *Kirk Pedersen*
DESIGN *Kirk Pedersen, Amanda Erlanson, Blaine Fontana*
ARTWORK *Andrew Hem*
PRODUCTION *Kirk Pedersen, Andrew Hem, The Goody Box Company*
DATE *2012*

Aura
Issue 2

〜〜〜〜〜〜〜〜〜〜

Specifications
Booklet
Card
Corrosion
Fluorescent ink
Foam
Handmade wooden box
Ink markers
Plywood
Reclaimed pine
Sandpapering
Softback magazine
Spray paint
Steel sheeting
Wood stain
Edition of 6

For London-based graphic designer and art director Simon Slater, the publication of issue 2 of his graffiti journal, *Aura*, was the perfect opportunity to produce a collector's edition. The print run for the journal was 1,000 copies; Slater printed an extra six for the collector's edition, and added a page at the front of each one explaining its status as part of a limited-edition box set.

The boxes themselves were made by hand. Fittingly, their steel covers were inspired by the weathered, graffiti-stained signal boxes often found on the side of railway lines. To ensure that each cover was slightly different, all six were placed side by side and painted by hand at the same time. Areas of the paint were then sandpapered, while parts of the exposed steel were made wet and allowed to rust, thus creating the desired weathered effect.

Inside the box, the journal is housed in dark-grey foam, but is hidden by a booklet. It is only by removing the booklet that the vibrant orange cover of the journal is revealed.

PUBLISHER *Simon Slater/LAKI 139, UK*
ART DIRECTION & DESIGN
Simon Slater/LAKI 139
DATE 2009

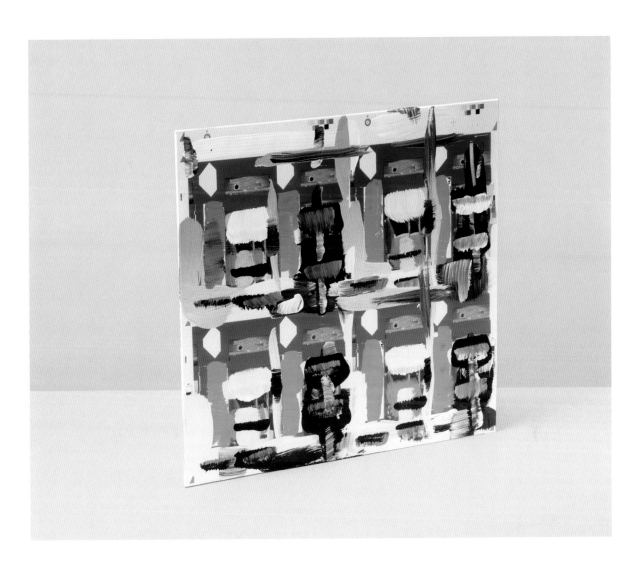

Wolfgang Voigt
Freiland Klaviermusik

Specifications
12" vinyl record
Acrylic paint
Hand painting
Hand-signed
Edition of 150

Wolfgang Voigt is a German producer and artist. Voigt's hand-painted sleeve for the limited edition of *Freiland Klaviermusik* is based on his own 'Tetra Pak' paintings, a series of works on flattened Tetra Paks.

—

PUBLISHER *Profan, Germany*
ART DIRECTION & DESIGN *Wolfgang Voigt*
PRODUCTION *Wolfgang Voigt*
DATE *2010*

Chris Ofili
Paradise by Night

Specifications

Black goatskin
Debossing
Embroidery
Feathered goatskin
Foil blocking
Hand-bound
Hand-dyed calfskin
Hand-printed lithography
Hardback book
Japanese book cloth
Letterpress printing
Metallic ink
Screen printing
Silk head and tail bands
Solander box
Zerkall mould-made paper
Edition of 40

Paradise by Night is the result of a collaboration between Turner Prize-winning British artist Chris Ofili and British writer, producer and DJ Charlie Dark. Based on a design by Ofili, the large-format book (52 × 36 cm/20½ × 14⅛ in.) consists of ten poems by a group of young poets and ten lithographs made by the artist in direct response to their work.

Owing to its largely handmade nature, each book is unique, from the hand-dyed calfskin used for the binding to the cover-mounted feathered onlays made from hand-coloured goatskin. The poems and text have been letterpress-printed, while the whole book has been hand-bound using fore-edge folds. Each book comes in a hand-made solander box covered in Japanese book cloth.

—

PUBLISHER *Léonie Booth-Clibborn (InBetween)/Paragon Press, UK*
DESIGN *Book Works Studio*
ARTWORKS *Chris Ofili*
PRODUCTION *Paupers Press, Book Works Studio, K2 Screen*
DATE *2010*

Lawrence Weiner
Tit as Tat

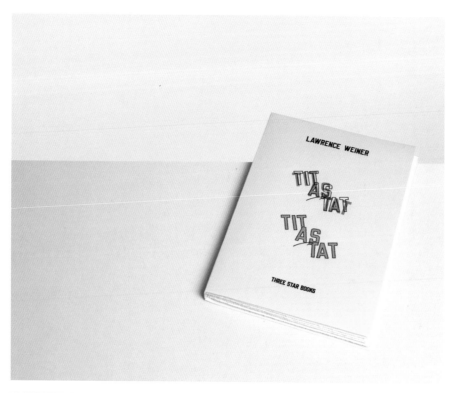

Specifications
5-colour letterpress printing
Cardboard
Hand-numbered
Hand-signed
Kraft paper
Slip case
Unbound book
Zerkall hammered paper
Edition of 30

In *Tit as Tat*, American conceptual artist Lawrence Weiner, best known for his text-based wall installations, explores the variations inherent to the letterpress process. 'The only thing about letterpress that interests me', he explains, 'is mis-registration ... Each time the press hits the paper it's a different impression.' Playing on the expression 'tit for tat', the book examines the way in which variations of the same thing, such as a mis-registered image, are essentially interchangeable.

The book itself consists of a series of Weiner's typographic compositions. These have been letterpress-printed on twelve sheets of paper, which, in turn, have been folded and loosely placed inside one of three differently coloured covers. The whole comes in a slip case made of cardboard and kraft paper.
—
PUBLISHER *Three Star Books, France*
ART DIRECTION & DESIGN *Lawrence Weiner*
ARTWORK *Lawrence Weiner*
LETTERPRESS *Polymers*
DATE *2013*

Coexistence is British photographer Stephen Gill's response to the now defunct steel-making industry in Dudelange, Luxembourg. Each copy of the special edition of the book features a unique hand-marbled cover made by Gill himself and hand-painted speckles on the paper edges. Contained in a cloth-covered box, the book also comes with a signed and numbered pigment print.

—

PUBLISHER *Nobody, UK/CNA Luxembourg*
ART DIRECTION *Stephen Gill*
DESIGN *Melanie Mues*
PHOTOGRAPHY *Stephen Gill*
PRODUCTION *Stephen Gill*
DATE *2012*

Stephen Gill
Coexistence

Specifications
Cloth-covered box
Foil blocking
Hand marbling
Hand-numbered
Hand-painted speckles
Hand-signed
Hardback book
Leather spine
Pigment print
Quarter binding
Solander box
Edition of 100

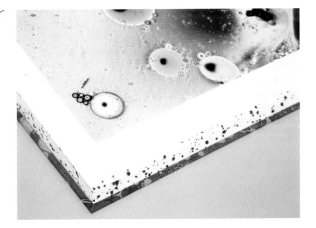

Meowtain
Hex/Piggyback Rider

Specifications
Acrylic paint
Foil stamping
Polycarbonate plastic
Square 8" vinyl record
Vintage letterpress type
Edition of 50

Every copy of *Hex/Piggyback Rider*, a single by American post-pop trio Meowtain, features a unique 'spin-painted' design. This was achieved by dropping paint on to each record as it was being spun on a turntable by means of a hand drill. Various paint-application techniques were experimented with, which led to a wide range of styles. Once all the records had been decorated, they were cut on a modified record lathe from the 1940s.

—

PUBLISHER *Piaptk Recordings, USA*
ART DIRECTION *Michael Dixon*
DESIGN *Michael Dixon, Elizabeth Fey, Dave Crager, Joel Davenport*
DATE *2013*

All Books is a collection of British conceptual artist Liam Gillick's major fictional texts, including *McNamara Papers*, *Ibuka* and *The Winter School*. For this special hardback edition, Gillick has hand-coloured the illustration on the dust jacket, giving each of the books in the edition an individual dimension. The slip case in which the book is supplied has only one transparent surface, which helps to frame the illustration.

—

PUBLISHER *Book Works, UK*
DESIGN *Liam Gillick*
ILLUSTRATION *M/M (Paris)*
PRODUCTION *Liam Gillick, De Keure, Book Works Studio*
DATE *2009*

Liam Gillick
All Books

Specifications
Hand colouring
Hand-signed
Hardback book
Letterpress printing
Perspex
Slip case
Spot colour
White book cloth
Zerkall mould-made paper
Edition of 30

EXTRAS

Collectible memorabilia, ultimate collectors' editions and sculptural objects incorporating digital technologies

The Flaming Lips
Michael Mayer
Nick Cave & The Bad Seeds
Björk
The Decemberists
Woody & Paul
Radiohead
Los Carpinteros
Brian Eno
Peter Gabriel
Thomas Mailaender
Sigur Rós
Nobuyoshi Araki
Jockum Nordström
Julian Cope
Qompendium Print Publication
Phish
The Shins
Peter Hook
Simon Norfolk
Paul McCartney & Wings
Pixies

Macklemore & Ryan Lewis
Heidi de Gier
Duran Duran
Taylor Deupree
Aiko Miyanaga
My Chemical Romance
Watergate
Bill Bruford
Oliver Jeffers
Lambchop
Paul & Linda McCartney
Rachel Whiteread
Will Oldham
Big Cosmos
Pachanga Boys
Tim Noble & Sue Webster
Broken Bells
Matthew Dear
Vogue Nederland
Neon Trees
Yayoi Kusama

THE

FLAMING

INTERVIEW : MATTHEW LEE

PHOTOGRAPH : EMILIANO GRANADO

LIPS

WAYNE COYNE is the lead singer, guitarist and songwriter for The Flaming Lips. Since its formation in Oklahoma in 1983, the band has released more than a dozen albums and become famous for its colourful, elaborate live shows. In 2011 the band produced a number of experimental releases, including *Gummy Song Skull* (see page 224), a four-song recording on a USB drive placed inside a 'gummy skull'.

Have you actually tried eating your gummy skull?

Well, I haven't eaten a whole one. I like gummy candy, but I don't eat lots of it because it sits in your gut and you regret it the next day. When we were researching it, we tried many different flavours and textures. The guy who made them for us is an expert. He's adamant about being the top gummy expert in the world.

Did you eat gummy candy as a child?

I don't think it was around when I was really small, but in the early 1990s we got a membership card for Sam's Club, one of those stores where you can buy wholesale junk like cases of Doritos and whole sides of beef, and we'd get five-pound bags of gummy sweets. And we'd watch movies and eat through the whole bag and then regret it later. I've always liked the idea that it's made from horse food or something, some weird bone substance.

Why make a skull?

Back in 1984, we were at my house taking photos of a skull I'd stolen from a high-school science class. One of the photos – of a guy coming out from behind a curtain holding this skull, his face spookily lit by a candle – became the cover of our first ever record, a self-titled EP [1984]. When we released the gummy skull in 2011, we were just out of our contract with Warner Bros., and had just started running our own record company again, so we revisited some of the earliest things we'd done.

Was it your idea or a band idea?

We all have similar, ridiculous tastes. In the beginning we were trying to make the skull out of bubblegum, but we couldn't find a bubblegum guy, and the gummy guy was very enthusiastic.

Many bands are producing collectible items to promote the physical, tactile object, as an alternative to downloads. Was that part of your thinking behind the skull?

I would be the first to stand up and say I'm glad we can download music. I encourage it. A lot of our fans can't afford to buy the gummy skull, but they can download the music for free. There's no way that we could prevent that from happening, and we don't want to. Obviously, it takes money away from people who used to earn a great living, and it's a catastrophe for them, but that's the truth of how the world works. I have to remind people that music has become free because people love music.

Your concerts are very participatory experiences. Did you make the skull with that sort of listener participation in mind?

I think it was George [Salisbury, The Flaming Lips' visual artist] who said, 'Why don't we make it so it doesn't last very long?' and we began to think that maybe we don't need to make things that are permanent. It's candy, so if you keep it in its plastic packaging, you could probably eat it in ten years from now. Some people don't eat it, they just cut the music out, but we do like the idea of people having to eat the skull to reach the EP.

Wasn't there also a marijuana-flavoured brain – a limited edition of the limited edition?

We did some shows at the Hollywood Forever Cemetery [in June 2011], and the limited-edition marijuana gummy skull was for that. If you can do whatever the fuck you want, you should do it.

Are you at a stage in your career where you can do whatever the fuck you want?

When we released our 24-hour song in a human skull [a 24-hour-long recording on a hard drive encased in an actual human skull; thirteen were put on sale at $5,000 each], that's something you're not normally able to do. But I live in Oklahoma City, and the guy who sells the human skulls also lives in Oklahoma City, and I think he's the only person in the world who could have done this for us. I mean, he literally has a fridge full of severed heads. I've had some doctor and lawyer friends help me, and I think the guy selling them to me cuts me some slack, but you would never be able to do blood records or human skulls through a giant corporation. So during the period when we weren't signed to Warner Bros., we tried to do lots of ridiculous, underground things.

'The people I've met who bought the skull ... are people who love having our music and art in their lives. They like the idea that we've done it, touched it, signed it, given love and care to it.'

Were any of these ideas unsuccessful?

We're trying to make an effects pedal for a guitar or keyboard that takes sounds randomly from the Internet: when you press buttons, you get totally random noises. Some of that just couldn't be done. We wouldn't want to put out something super-expensive – we're not a manufacturing company. And the gummy skulls were a one-off. We had a couple of hundred delivered, all at the same time, and it's Oklahoma in July and extremely hot ... I like to experiment but I'm not a candy store. Now we're signed to a record company again, we're more limited in what we can do.

Have digital downloads changed the way you approach music?

Digital is so cheap and immediate. When we're working, there are always little things that we send back and forth to one another, something we couldn't do before. We used to spend days shipping giant email files to each other. I love being able to do things quickly. I don't think MP3s are the enemy of music. Some people obsess over quality, but some things sound more interesting at a lower quality. It's not better or worse, it's just different.

What type of person is buying the gummy skull?

We're not trying to attract collectors, the kind of people who think they can hold on to it for five years and then sell it at a big profit. The people I've met who bought it – and I delivered some of the skulls myself – are people who love having our music and art in their lives. They like the idea that we've done it, touched it, signed it, given love and care to it, and they know that it represents a time in their lives and a time in ours. *Wayne Coyne was photographed at Terminal 5, New York, USA*

The Flaming Lips
Gummy Song Skull

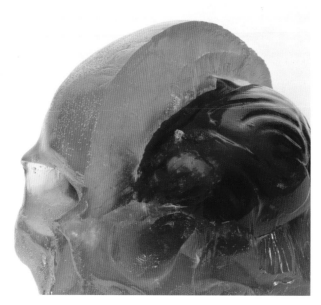

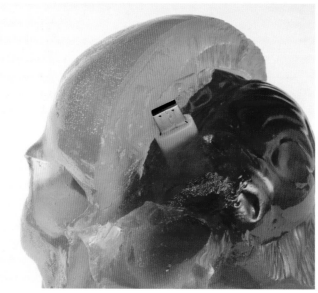

Specifications
Citric acid
Flavouring
Food colouring
Gelatin
Glucose syrup
Starch
Sugar
USB drive

American alternative rock band The Flaming Lips recorded the *Gummy Song Skull* EP as part of 'The Flaming Lips 2011', a year-long series of monthly music releases. The four-song EP takes the form of a USB drive inside a brain-shaped piece of gummy candy that is itself encased in a life-size gummy skull. In order to retrieve the USB, you have to eat at least a portion of the skull.

After a failed attempt to make the skull themselves, the band turned to Derek Lawson, CEO of Giant Gummy Bears. 'We found him online,' explains lead singer Wayne Coyne, 'and we called him up and said, "Hey, we want to do this life-size skull." And then we said, "We're in this band called The Flaming Lips." And he was like, "Woah, I'm a huge fan." So there was a kind of serendipity to finding someone who's a freak and a fan.'

—

PUBLISHER *Lovely Sorts of Death, USA*
ART DIRECTION *Wayne Coyne, George Salisbury (Delo Creative)*
PRODUCTION *Derek Lawson*
DATE *2011*

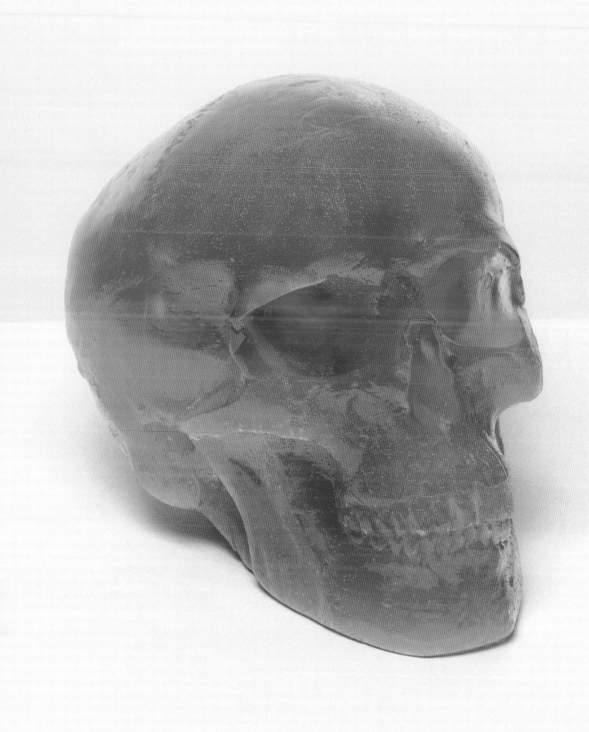

Michael Mayer
Mantasy

++++++++++++++

Specifications
2 12" vinyl records
Rigid board
Silk

The limited edition of *Mantasy*, the second album by German producer, remixer and DJ Michael Mayer, comes with a silk scarf. The design of both the scarf and the record sleeve is based on the art of producer and artist Wolfgang Voigt (see page 211), specifically his 'digital painting' series *Zukunft Ohne Menschen* (Future without humans).

—

PUBLISHER *Kompakt, Germany*
ART DIRECTION & DESIGN *Wolfgang Voigt*
DATE *2012*

The super-deluxe edition of *Push the Sky Away*, the fifteenth studio album by Nick Cave & The Bad Seeds, was a collaboration between Cave himself and Tom Hingston Studio in London. A key component of the box set is a notebook containing the reproduced contents of Cave's own notebooks. In what was a highly complex print project, the studio painstakingly reproduced every hand-glued note, typewritten insertion and rubber stamp from the original notebooks. Each element was scanned, tidied up and combined with the others by hand.

—

PUBLISHER *Bad Seed Ltd in partnership with Kobalt Label Services, UK*
ART DIRECTION & DESIGN *Nick Cave, Tom Hingston Studio*
PHOTOGRAPHY *Dominique Issermann*
ILLUSTRATION *Nick Cave*
PRODUCTION *Think Tank Media*
DATE *2013*

Specifications

2 7" vinyl records
12" vinyl record
CD
Certificate of authenticity
Clothbound box
Debossing
DVD
Foil blocking
Gold foil
Hand finishing
Hardback notebook
Linen book cloth
Rigid board
Rubber band
Rubber stamps
Tipped-on artwork
Tipped-in pages

Nick Cave & The Bad Seeds
Push the Sky Away

Björk
Biophilia

Specifications
10 tuning forks
CD
Certificate of authenticity
Chrome plate
Foil blocking
Hardback book
Hinged-lid case
Lacquer
Lenticular panel
Oak
Screen printing
Silk ribbon
Thread sewing
Edition of 200

Partly recorded on an iPad, and encompassing live performances and a series of apps, *Biophilia* is Björk's eighth full-length album. The 'ultimate art edition' of the record consists of a wooden box containing, among other things, a hardback book and ten custom-made tuning forks, each of which is tuned to a different track from the album.

—

PUBLISHER *One Little Indian Records, UK*
ART DIRECTION *M/M (Paris)*
ILLUSTRATION *M/M (Paris)*
PHOTOGRAPHY *Inez van Lamsweerde, Vinoodh Matadin*
PRODUCTION *Daniel Mason (Something Else)*
DATE *2011*

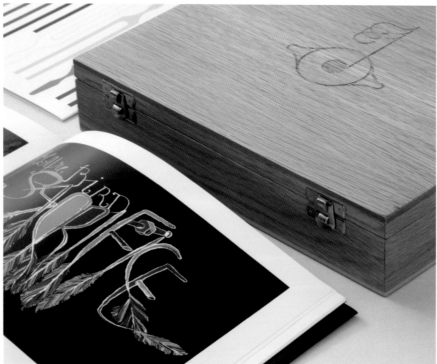

The Decemberists
The King Is Dead

Specifications

12" vinyl record
Blotter paper
CD
DVD
Embossing
Foil stamping
Giclee print
Hardback book
Linen book cloth
Metallic ink
Satin ribbon
Solander box
Unique Polaroid photo
Edition of 2,500

This deluxe edition of *The King Is Dead*, the sixth studio album by American indie folk-rock band The Decemberists, includes an original Polaroid taken by American photographer Autumn de Wilde. Also included is a hardback book featuring a selection of de Wilde's other Polaroids of the band and artwork by Decemberists' illustrator-in-residence Carson Ellis.
—

PUBLISHER *Capitol Records, USA*
DESIGN *Jeri Heiden (Smog Design Inc.)*
PHOTOGRAPHY *Autumn de Wilde*
ILLUSTRATION *Carson Ellis*
PRODUCTION *Multi Packaging Solutions*
DATE *2011*

Woody & Paul
Heroes and Zeroes: D/struct Edition

++++++++++++++++

Specifications
Destroyed vinyl
Digital printing
Laser cutting
Plastic

This highly unusual edition of Dutch band Woody & Paul's album *Heroes and Zeroes* (see page 116) is part of the D/struct project. According to its initiators, Dutch graphic designer Lucas Maassen and Dutch design studio Raw Color, D/struct was established to examine three interrelated issues: the function of physical products in a largely digital world, how such products could be acquired digitally, and what this form of retail might mean for the consumer. The result was an entirely new kind of product.

Each item in the D/struct 'range' consists of a pulverized version of one of sixty plastic goods – in this case, a copy of *Heroes and Zeroes* – in a plastic bag. In addition, the buyer also receives a download code that allows them to access a complete high-resolution 3D scan of the original object. This scan, says the D/struct website, enables the buyer 'to reconstruct another version – or endlessly come up with other versions and variations – of the shattered original using his own 3D printer'.
—

PUBLISHER *Woody & Paul, The Netherlands*
ART DIRECTION & DESIGN *Raw Color, Lucas Maassen*
PRODUCTION *Raw Color, Lucas Maassen*
DATE *2011*

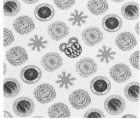

Radiohead
The King of Limbs

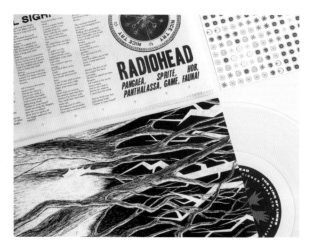

Specifications
2 clear 10" vinyl records
32-page newspaper
CD
Corrugated cardboard
Gloss UV varnish
Grain embossing
Matt UV varnish
Newsprint
Oxo-degradable polythene
Perforation

For the special 'newspaper' edition of *The King of Limbs*, Radiohead's eighth studio album, long-serving Radiohead collaborator Stanley Donwood wanted to create something 'in a state of flux', choosing newsprint for its ephemeral nature. He also took inspiration from a selection of real publications, including a collection of radical 1960s newspapers and magazines found at bassist Colin Greenwood's house, and weekend broadsheets. 'I wanted to do something really annoying', explains Donwood, 'something with all these crappy bits of floppy, glossy paper.'

—

PUBLISHER *Radiohead, UK*
ART DIRECTION *Stanley Donwood*
ARTWORK *Stanley Donwood*
PRODUCTION *Clear Sound and Vision*
DATE *2011*

Los Carpinteros
Handwork: Constructing the World

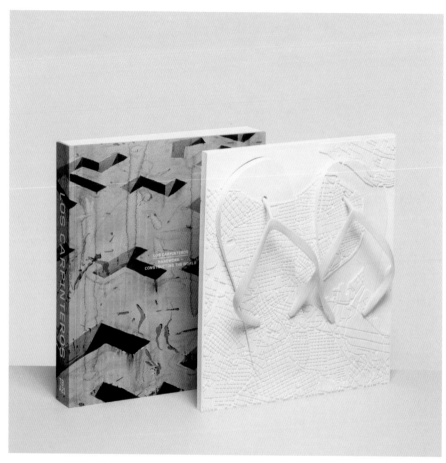

┼┼┼┼┼┼┼┼┼┼┼┼

Specifications
Elastomer
Hardback book
Injection-moulded flip flops
PVC
White cardboard box
Edition of 200

The special edition of *Handwork: Constructing the World*, a catalogue of works by Los Carpinteros, comes with a pair of injection-moulded flip flops. Imprinted with a street map of old Havana, the shoes refer to earlier works by the Cuban art collective, including a series of drawings and *Sandalia* (2004), rapid-prototyped flip flops bearing a 3D map of the city's neighbourhoods.

The main challenge faced by the project's designers, Vienna-based studio Schienerl, was to create a product that was both a well-defined 3D map and a comfortable pair of shoes. The solution lay in finding the correct ratio of the base elastomer material to the white colouring agent. 'It quickly began to feel like alchemy', explains studio founder Christian Schienerl. 'In the end, we had cooked up "white gold".'
—

PUBLISHER *Verlag der Buchhandlung Walther König, Germany*
EDITORS *Daniela Zyman, Gudrun Ankele (Thyssen-Bornemisza Art Contemporary)*
ART DIRECTION & DESIGN *Christian Schienerl (Schienerl D/AD)*
PRODUCTION *Holzhausen Druck GmbH, Zahradka (flip flops)*
DATE *2011*

Brian Eno
Small Craft on a Milk Sea

+++++++++++++++

Specifications
2 12" vinyl records
2 CDs
Birch paper
Embedded copper plate
Etching
Foil blocking
Hand-numbered
Hand-signed
Hardback gatefold sleeve
Screen printing
Slip case
Unique artwork
Edition of 250

This collector's edition of *Small Craft on a Milk Sea*, British musician and producer Brian Eno's first album for Warp, includes a unique screen print. Produced using a customized screen-printing process that references Eno's work in other areas of 'generative' art, each print features elements created by both Eno and his long-time visual collaborator, Nick Robertson.

—

PUBLISHER *Warp, UK*
ART DIRECTION *Nick Robertson*
DESIGN *Wordsalad*
PRODUCTION *James Burton (Warp), Daniel Mason (Something Else)*
DATE *2010*

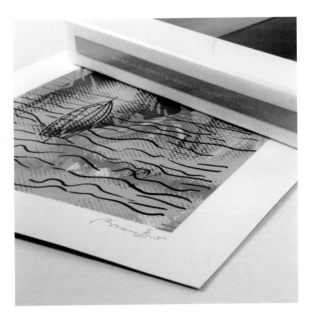

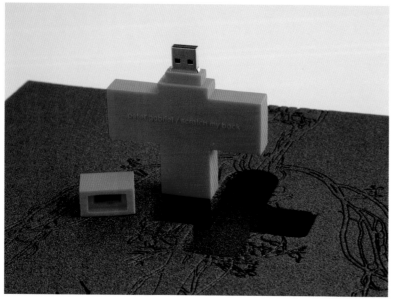

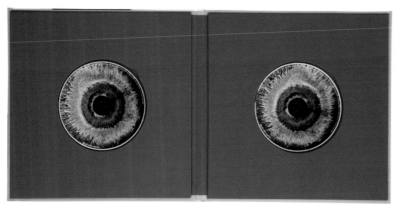

Peter Gabriel
Scratch My Back

Specifications
2 CDs
Art print
Blood-red 12" vinyl record
Certificate of authenticity
Foam tray
Foil blocking
Gloss lamination
Hand-numbered
Hand-signed
Hardback CD wallet
Laser engraving
Lift-off-lid box
Photographic print
Production-credits panel
USB drive
Edition of 500

Scratch My Back, an album of cover versions by British musician Peter Gabriel, was conceived as part of a two-album project. Its companion record, *And I'll Scratch Yours* (2013), features specially recorded versions of Gabriel's songs by artists covered in *Scratch My Back*.

For the special edition of the album, designer Marc Bessant had a clear idea of what he hoped to achieve: 'I wanted the images, colours and materials to be seductive, sensual, to have a relationship with one another, to stand up as individual parts yet work best as a whole.' He was particularly interested in working with micrographs (photographs taken through a microscope), and at looking at 'what goes on inside us'.

The finished box set features the work of British scientific photographer Steve Gschmeissner, including micrographs of red blood cells and a jagged, broken fingernail. This, explains Bessant, 'gives us our title served on a slightly skewed but gently warmed plate'.

—

PUBLISHER *Real World*, UK
ART DIRECTION & DESIGN *Marc Bessant*
PHOTOGRAPHY *Steve Gschmeissner, Nadav Kander*
PRODUCTION *Daniel Mason (Something Else)*
DATE *2010*

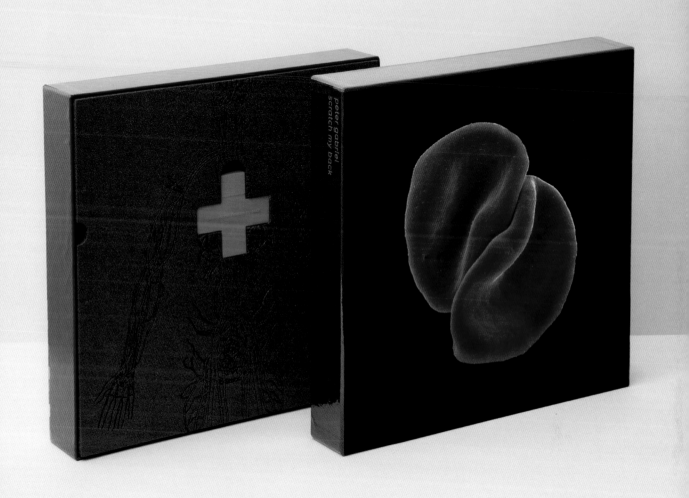

Thomas Mailaender
Cathedral Cars

Specifications
Art print
Booklet
Gloss lamination
Handmade plastic bag
Hand-numbered
Hand-signed
Hardback book
Screen printing
Silver foil blocking
Steel
Edition of 50

The limited edition of *Cathedral Cars* was the result of a close collaboration between French artist Thomas Mailaender and the book's publishers, Paris-based RVB Books. It was decided that the exclusive screen print should be made on steel, in reference to the content of the book: photographs of vehicles, or 'cathedral cars', overloaded with the belongings of North African migrants arriving in Europe. The bag in which the large-format book (38 × 30 cm/15 × 11¾ in.) is supplied was handmade in honour of the similar bags found in almost all the photos. A second limited edition features gold rather than silver foil blocking.
—

PUBLISHER *RVB Books, France*
ART DIRECTION *Thomas Mailaender, Rémi Faucheux*
DESIGN *Thomas Mailaender*
PHOTOGRAPHY *Thomas Mailaender*
PRODUCTION *Tien Wah Press*
DATE *2012*

Inni comprises both the first-ever live album by Sigur Rós and the second film of the Icelandic band performing live, in this case at London's Alexandra Palace in November 2008. Directed by Vincent Morisset, the dark, claustrophobic film was originally shot on HD digital. It was then transferred to 16mm stock before being projected and re-filmed, sometimes through glass and other objects to give a strongly impressionistic look.

Among the various extras included in the collector's edition of *Inni* was a unique artefact from the concerts: a hand-cut piece of the band's stage costumes. Also included were ten sheets of light-sensitive paper. A reference to Morisset's use of light and shadow, the paper could be used by fans to create their own images as part of an online competition.
—

PUBLISHER *Krunk, UK*
ART DIRECTION & DESIGN *Sarah Hopper*
PHOTOGRAPHY *Vincent Morisset,*
Karl Lemieux
ILLUSTRATION *Caroline Robert*
PRODUCTION *Modo*
DATE *2011*

Sigur Rós
Inni

Specifications
2 CDs
4-panel CD slitpack
4 photographic prints
Black opaque envelope
Blu-ray disc
Coloured 7" vinyl record
DVD
Enamel badge
Etching
Lift-off-lid box
Light-sensitive paper
Unique artefact

Nobuyoshi Araki
Bondage: Art Edition

++++++++++++++++++++++++++++++++++

Specifications
3 paperback books
Bamboo box
Blind embossing
Fore-edge folds
Hand-numbered
Hand-signed
Japanese stab binding
Laser engraving
Photographic print
Traditional kimono fabric
Edition of 150

The Japanese art of erotic bondage, *kinbaku-bi* (literally, the beauty of tight binding), has long fascinated Japanese photographer Nobuyoshi Araki. This three-volume collection of Araki's bondage photography – featuring images chosen by Araki himself, and accompanied by one of three Araki prints – incorporates an array of design features intended to reflect the culture, heritage and vision of the erotic content.

Each volume in the collection consists of a series of printed leaves that have been folded at the fore-edge and bound together using stab binding. (The insides of the leaves have been printed with a Pantone red.) The cover page of each volume has been blind embossed with the collection's title and a series of rope marks, suggesting the marks left on the skin of Araki's models. The box in which the three volumes are housed has been laser-engraved with the title, and both lined with and secured by kimono fabric. In a further nod to Japanese tradition, all texts have been hand-written by Araki.

—

PUBLISHER *TASCHEN, Germany*
ART DIRECTION & DESIGN
Andy Disl, Birgit Eichwede (Sense/Net)
PHOTOGRAPHY *Nobuyoshi Araki*
PRODUCTION *Frank Goerhardt,
Javier Bone-Carbone, Stefan Klatte*
DATE *2012*

Jockum Nordström
Barnteckningar och dikter på anhalten före döden

Specifications
Artist's bookplate
Cardboard sculpture
Hand-numbered
Hand-signed
Hardback book

Barnteckningar ... is Swedish artist Jockum Nordström's contribution to 'Edition Ex Libris', a series of limited-edition reprints. Each book in the series has been chosen by an internationally acclaimed artist as having had a particular impact on their life and work; Nordström's choice is the Swedish edition of a collection of drawings and poems made by children imprisoned in Terezín Concentration Camp during the Second World War. Significantly, each artist is asked to provide their chosen reprint with a newly designed cover or dust jacket and a personalized bookplate in a form of their choosing. A collector's edition of each book comes with an additional, larger-format work by the artist; in Nordström's case, this takes the form of a cardboard sculpture.

—

PUBLISHER *Salon Verlag & Edition, Germany*
DESIGN *Jockum Nordström*
ILLUSTRATION *Children from Terezín Concentration Camp*
DATE *2013*

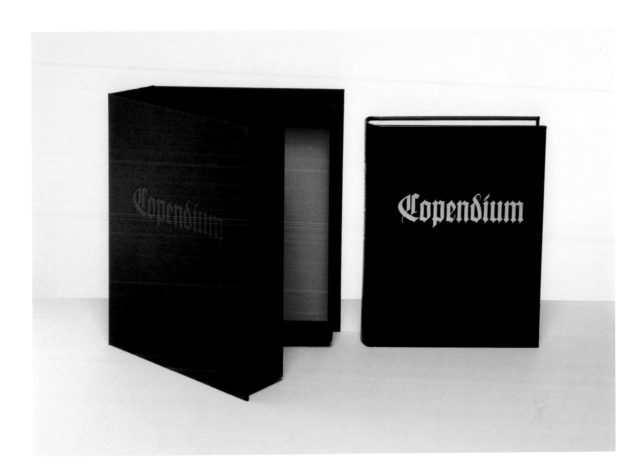

Written by British musician, author and musicologist Julian Cope, *Copendium* is a collection of album reviews that, taken as a whole, provide an alternative history of the last six decades of popular music. This limited edition of the book is accompanied by three sampler CDs; compiled by Cope himself, they are intended to be listened to while reading the book. The result, according to the publishers, 'is a feast of obscure and neglected masterworks', from Krautrock, motorik and post-punk to stoner, jazz and 'hair metal'.

—

PUBLISHER *Faber and Faber, UK*
DESIGN *Eleanor Crow (Faber and Faber)*
TYPOGRAPHY *Dave Watkins (Faber and Faber)*
PRODUCTION *Jack Murphy (Faber and Faber), Lachenmaier GmbH*
DATE *2012*

Julian Cope
Copendium

┼┼┼┼┼┼┼┼┼┼┼┼┼┼┼┼┼┼┼

Specifications
3 CDs
Black bookcalf leather
Blind blocking
'Blood splatter' endpapers
Handmade paper
Hand-numbered
Hand-signed
Hardback book
Red ribbon marker
Red/white head and tail bands
Silver foil blocking
Solander box
Edition of 300

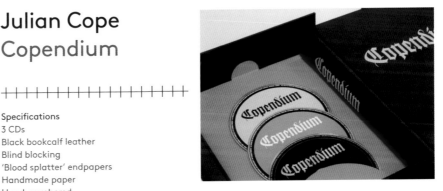

Qompendium Print Publication
Volume 1

++++++++++++++++++++++++++++++++

Specifications
2 T-shirts
5 different covers
Box
Cardboard
Custom-dyed paper
Embossing
Foil blocking
Luxury skincare product
Paperback book
Poster set
Screen printing
Set of printed questions
Edition of 357

According to its website, Qompendium is 'an evolving and ever-changing platform for philosophy, art, culture and science, represented by a series of print publications: magazines, books and monographs'. Central to Qompendium's various publications is an emphasis on high design and production values, including the use of different paper stocks, printing inks and finishing techniques.

Such values are especially apparent in the collector's edition of the first volume of *Qompendium Print Publication*, a magazine composed of pictorial essays, interviews and editorials. This first volume covers such diverse subjects as the fortieth anniversary of the first Moon landings, artificial intelligence and Michael Jackson memorabilia.

Supplied in a cardboard box, the magazine is accompanied by numerous extras. These include a set of posters made from running sheets taken from the printing of the magazine; a set of screen-printed cards featuring questions posed by American astrophysicist Neil deGrasse Tyson; an interview with Nick Sagan, son of astronomer Carl; and two T-shirts with designs inspired by philosophy and astronomy. To reflect the astronomical content of the magazine, the front of the box has been screen-printed with a selection of scientific illustrations taken from the era of Copernicus and the Age of Enlightenment.

—
PUBLISHER *Lloyd & Associates GmbH, Germany*
CREATIVE DIRECTION *Kimberly Lloyd*
ART DIRECTION *Kimberly Lloyd, Johannes Spitzer*
DESIGN *Kimberly Lloyd, Johannes Spitzer*
PHOTOGRAPHY *Lyn Balzer, Valérie Belim, Laurence Ellis, Emir Eralp, Deborah Feingold, Dominik Gigler, Douglas Kirkland, Tony Perkins, Daniel Stier, Andy Warhol, Ben Watts, Christian Weber, Doug Wilson, Per Zennström et al.*
ILLUSTRATION *Paul Pope*
PRODUCTION *Lloyd & Associates GmbH*
DATE *2009*

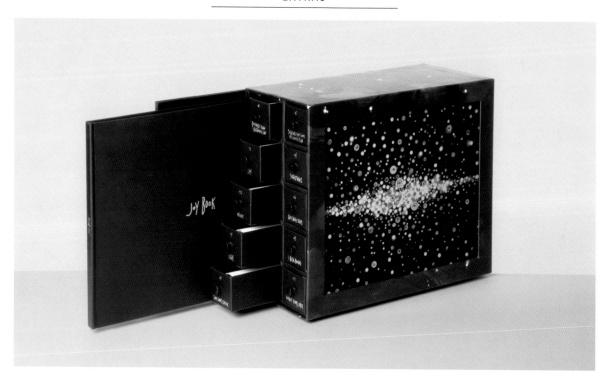

When Denver-based Varnish Studio Inc. was approached to design *Joy Box* – the special edition of *Joy*, the eleventh official studio album by American rock band Phish – there was only one requirement. The band wanted to hire ten of their favourite illustrators to create ten posters, one for each of the album's ten tracks. The challenge for Varnish was to find a way of safely packaging these posters. The solution was a system of ten drawers hidden inside a hinged box, with each poster rolled up inside one of the drawers. The box itself is intended to suggest a block of outer space.

—

PUBLISHER *Jemp Records, USA/Phish*
ART DIRECTION & DESIGN
Matt Taylor (Varnish Studio Inc.)
PHOTOGRAPHY *Danny Clinch*
ILLUSTRATION *Fred Tomaselli (box cover),*
Matt Taylor (book)
POSTER DESIGN *Deanne Cheuk, Mario Hugo, Matt Huynh, Micah Lindberg, Grady McFerrin, Mike Perry, Jim Pollock, Luke Ramsey, Nikolav Savaliev, Alex Trochut*
PRODUCTION *Color Service Inc.*
DATE *2009*

Phish
Joy Box

┼┼┼┼┼┼┼┼┼┼┼┼┼┼┼┼┼┼┼┼┼

Specifications
2 CDs
10 posters
APET window
Black aluminium drawer-pull
Box
Chipboard
DVD
Embossing
Hardback book
Lithograph
Magnetic side flap
Metallic-silver foil stamping
Silk ribbon
Spot metallic silver

Specifications
¼" reel-to-reel tape
Numbered box
Postcards

Created by American designer
and illustrator Jacob Escobedo,
the cover for *Port of Morrow* was
inspired by Native American
imagery, kachina dolls (small
carved figures representing the
deified ancestral spirits found
in Pueblo Indian mythology)
and psychedelic book covers
from Eastern Europe. On closer
inspection, the mountain forms
the silhouette of a young girl,
an image inspired by lyrics
taken from the album's title
track. This special edition of the
album, the American indie rock
band's fourth, is supplied on
¼" reel-to-reel tape. For those
without the necessary audio
equipment to play the tape, the
album also comes with a code
enabling the buyer to download
a digital version.

—

PUBLISHER *Columbia Records, USA*
ART DIRECTION *Jacob Escobedo*
ILLUSTRATION *Jacob Escobedo*
DATE *2012*

The Shins
Port of Morrow

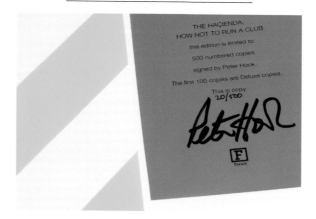

Peter Hook

The Haçienda:
How Not to Run a Club

Specifications
Art print
Black foil stamping
Black silk ribbon
Canadian maple
Die cutting
Fine black rubber
Hand-bound
Hand feathering
Hand-numbered
Hand-signed
Hardback book
Laser etching
Pieces of Haçienda interior
Screen printing
Solander box
Stainless steel
Tipped-in pages
Yellow 10" vinyl record
Edition of 100

In *The Haçienda: How Not to Run a Club*, legendary bass-player Peter Hook recounts his experiences of Manchester's most iconic nightclub, of which he was a co-owner. Linking the various elements of this deluxe edition are materials and graphics redolent of the Haçienda itself: maple for the dance floor and chevrons for everywhere else. Among the added extras are actual pieces of the club's interior, including a section of the original granite bar top engraved with 'FAC51', the club's number in the catalogue of co-financier Factory Records.

PUBLISHER *Foruli, UK*
ART DIRECTION & DESIGN *Andy Vella*
ILLUSTRATION *Andy Vella*
DATE *2011*

Simon Norfolk
Bleed

Specifications

Acrylic block
Black Cialux book cloth
Black Imitlin
Foil stamping
Gloss lamination
Gloss varnish
Hand-numbered
Hand-signed
Hardback book
High-impact foam
Matt lamination
Matt varnish
Photographic print
Slip case
Edition of 50

During the Bosnian War (1992–95), Serbian fighters would return to the mass graves of their civilian victims and re-bury the bodies in an attempt to hide them from the eyes of the world. In *Bleed*, Nigerian-born photographer Simon Norfolk explores the often icy landscapes that hid these 'secondary' mass graves, as well as the evidence rooms of the UN investigators. The 'image block' – a 33 × 26.4-cm (13 × 10⅜-in.) print encased in acrylic – included with the limited edition was chosen as a metaphor for a block of ice within which a secret is held.

—

PUBLISHER *Dewi Lewis Publishing, UK*
ART DIRECTION & DESIGN *Dewi Lewis, Simon Norfolk*
PHOTOGRAPHY *Simon Norfolk*
PRODUCTION *EBS Verona, Spectrum, J. T. Sawyer & Co. Ltd*
DATE *2005*

Paul McCartney & Wings
Wings over America

++++++++++++

Specifications
2 paperback books
2 reproduction fabric stickers
3 CDs
3 photographic prints
6 reproduction tickets
Book cloth
Die cutting
DVD
Embossing
End-of-tour party invitations
Foil blocking
Hardback book
Holographic foil
PVC
Screen printing
Set list
Slip case
Stochastic printing
Synthetic-leather-bound book
Tour programme

Wings over America, the second super-deluxe release in the Paul McCartney Archive Collection (see also page 267), is intended to encapsulate the spirit of the band's 1976 tour of the United States. Included in the box set is a remastered version of the original 1976 album plus numerous extras. Eighteen different types of paper were used in the production of the various components, while the box itself has been designed to resemble a decorated flight case. In 2014 the box set won the Grammy Award for Best Boxed or Special Limited Edition Package.

—

PUBLISHER *MPL/Concord/Universal Music, UK*
ART DIRECTION & DESIGN *Yes*
CREATIVE CONSULTANT *Roger Huggett*
ORIGINAL DESIGN *MPL, Hipgnosis, Richard Evans, Geoff Halpin*
PHOTOGRAPHY *Linda McCartney, Robert Ellis, Humphrey Ocean, Aubrey Powell, Pamela Keats*
ILLUSTRATION *Humphrey Ocean, George Hardie*
ORIGINAL ARTWORK *Richard Manning, Humphrey Ocean*
PRINT PRODUCTION *Brian Schuman*
PRODUCTION *MPL*
DATE *2013*

Pixies
Minotaur

+++++++++++++

Specifications
2 double-sided posters
2 hardback books
5 12" vinyl records
5 gold-plated CDs
Blu-ray disc
Custom-designed folio
Debossing
DVD
Faux fur
Felt
Giclee print
Hand-numbered
Hand-signed
Oversized lift-off-lid box
Screen printing

Asked to describe the limited-edition box set of *Minotaur*, Pixies drummer David Lovering said, 'It's beyond my expectations. I thought it was going to be your typical box set, but it's monstrous. I've never seen anything like it.' Weighing in at 11.3 kilograms (25 lb), and standing more than half a metre (1½ ft) tall, the limited edition of *Minotaur* is the definitive Pixies collector's piece.

The whole package was put together by British graphic designer Vaughan Oliver, who, in conjunction with British photographer Simon Larbalestier, created the artwork for all five Pixies' studio albums – each of which is included here, on CD and vinyl. Each copy of the limited edition has been hand-signed by Oliver and every member of the band. In addition, a randomly selected 25 of the 3,000 made were supplied with test pressings of the vinyl albums.

—

PUBLISHER *Artist in Residence, USA*
ART DIRECTION & DESIGN
Vaughan Oliver (v23)
PHOTOGRAPHY *Simon Larbalestier*
ILLUSTRATION *Students of the UCA, Epsom*
PRODUCTION *Tien Wah Press*
DATE *2009*

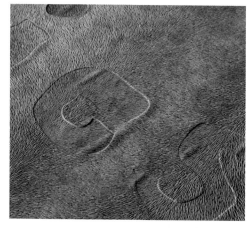

Macklemore & Ryan Lewis
The Heist

+++++++++++++++++

Specifications
2-piece box
19 art cards
Black Pellaq Croco
CD
Foil stamping
Gloss aqueous coating
Gold foil
Metallic-gold tissue paper

With *The Heist*, an album by American rapper–producer duo Macklemore & Ryan Lewis, the duo's manager, Zach Quillen, felt it was essential to create a special edition that would offer people a more in-depth experience. 'We've seen how powerful a strong marriage between music and the visual arts can be,' he explains, 'so we decided to create a high-end piece that would encourage a young generation to experience the project in a physical form.'

—

PUBLISHER *Macklemore & Ryan Lewis, USA*
ART DIRECTION *Ben Haggerty, Ryan Lewis, Zach Quillen, Tricia Davis*
DESIGN *Ryan Lewis*
ARTWORK *Ben Haggerty, Ryan Lewis, Kyle Johnson, Thig Nat, Dan Black, Jordan Nicholson, Derek Erdman, Jenna Derosa, Stacey Rozich, Zoe Rain Baxter, Jason Koenig, Bobby Silver*
PRODUCTION *Copy Cats Media*
DATE *2012*

Heidi de Gier
A Falling Horizon

Specifications
2 photographic prints
Handmade box
Hand-numbered
Hand-signed
Hardback book
Hessian book cloth
iPod Shuffle
Edition of 10

The Sophiapolder is a small island in the river Noord, not far from Rotterdam. For years, Heidi de Gier's aunt and her children had been running a sheep farm on the island. Every morning they would row across the river to take care of the animals. When the Dutch photographer discovered that the family would have to leave their home to make way for a freshwater tidal marsh, she began to photograph life on the farm. The special edition of the resulting book, *A Falling Horizon*, includes two signed and numbered photographic prints and an iPod Shuffle loaded with the soundscapes of the island.

—

PUBLISHER *Fw: Publishers, The Netherlands*
DESIGN *Hans Gremmen*
PHOTOGRAPHY *Heidi de Gier*
PRODUCTION *Drukkerij Raddraaier*
YEAR *2011*

Duran Duran
All You Need Is Now

Specifications
2 booklets
5 12" vinyl records
Die cutting
Hand-numbered
Hand-signed
Perspex box
Silver foil
Silver mirrored surface paper
Spot UV varnish
Edition of 500

Produced by celebrated British musician, DJ and producer Mark Ronson, *All You Need Is Now* is Duran Duran's thirteenth studio album. Begun in the spring of 2009, at London's Sphere Studios, the album has been described by Ronson as 'the imaginary follow-up to *Rio* [the band's second album] that never was'. This limited-edition box set includes not only a double-vinyl version of *All You Need Is Now* but also an LP of bonus tracks and two discs of remixes.

The design of the box set is very much in keeping with the band's reputation for combining pop music with art and fashion. Each of the five record sleeves features exclusive artwork by British artist Clunie Reid; further examples of Reid's cover designs appear in one of the two booklets included with the box set. The whole package comes in a clear-fronted Perspex slip case, which can be used as a frame for the sleeve artwork.

—

PUBLISHER *The Vinyl Factory, UK*
ART DIRECTION & DESIGN *Rory McCartney, The Vinyl Factory*
PHOTOGRAPHY *Clunie Reid*
ILLUSTRATION *Clunie Reid*
PRODUCTION *The Vinyl Factory*
YEAR *2011*

Taylor Deupree
Faint

Specifications
2 CDs
12 photographs
Lift-off-lid box
Matt varnish
Vellum

Faint is an audio/visual project by American musician and photographer Taylor Deupree, the subject of which is the moment of time between waking and sleep. The deluxe edition includes two CDs and twelve photographs taken by Deupree with a hand-built, plastic 35mm camera. The photographs themselves, of landscapes and the sky, were created using multiple exposures.

—
PUBLISHER *12k, USA*
ART DIRECTION & DESIGN *Taylor Deupree*
PHOTOGRAPHY *Taylor Deupree*
ILLUSTRATION *DAG*
PRODUCTION *Bellwether Manufacturing*
DATE *2012*

Japanese artist Aiko Miyanaga creates everyday objects from such organic substances as naphthalene (used in mothballs) and salt. This book, the artist's first monograph, was published on the occasion of her solo exhibition at the National Museum of Art, Osaka. Each copy of the special edition has a small, original artwork embedded in its cover: a jigsaw piece enclosed in transparent resin. In common with the artist's other work, the jigsaw piece will eventually degrade – should a covered hole in the resin be exposed to the air.

—

PUBLISHER *Seigensha Art Publishing Inc./ Mizuma Art Gallery, Japan*
ART DIRECTION & DESIGN *Toyonaga Seiji*
PHOTOGRAPHY *Toyonaga Seiji, Omote Nobutada*
PRODUCTION *Taiwa Print Co. Ltd*
DATE *2012*

Specifications
Certificate of authenticity
Hand-numbered
Hand-signed
Hardback book
Naphthalene
Resin
Silk ribbon
Unique artwork
Edition of 50

Aiko Miyanaga
Nakasora

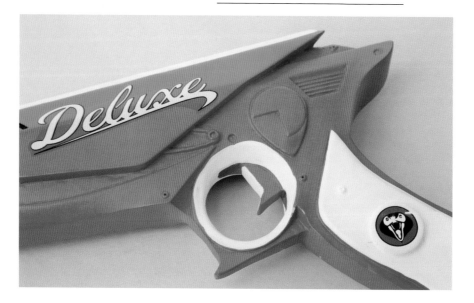

My Chemical Romance
Danger Days: The True Lives of the Fabulous Killjoys

Specifications
2 CDs
Acrylic stand
Booklet
Custom box with sleeve
Custom multicolour decals
Die cutting
Etched metal plaque
Hand-painted plastic mask
Resin-moulded toy gun
Spot foil stamping
Wooden beads

Danger Days, the final album by American alternative rock band My Chemical Romance, is set in a futuristic, dystopian California of the band's own imagining. The year is 2019, and one corporation, Better Living Industries, controls and manufactures all goods, products and services, including weapons. As the Fabulous Killjoys, My Chemical Romance must fight to keep a little girl – who has something that BLI wants – out of the corporation's evil clutches.

The special edition of the album comes with a series of objects designed to evoke this dystopic world. Each box includes one of four different model ray guns, as used by the band in the album's videos; a colour-coordinated mask; a set of 'bad luck' beads, also from the videos; an acrylic stand for the gun; an art book; a CD copy of the album; and an exclusive EP.

—

PUBLISHER *Warner Bros. Records, USA*
ART DIRECTION *Matt Taylor (Varnish Studio Inc.), Gerard Way, Ellen Wakayama*
DESIGN *Matt Taylor, Anna Tes*
PHOTOGRAPHY *Neil Krug, Greg Watermann, Frank Iero, Matt Taylor*
PRODUCTION *D'Andrea Graphics, Jack Nadel International*
DATE *2010*

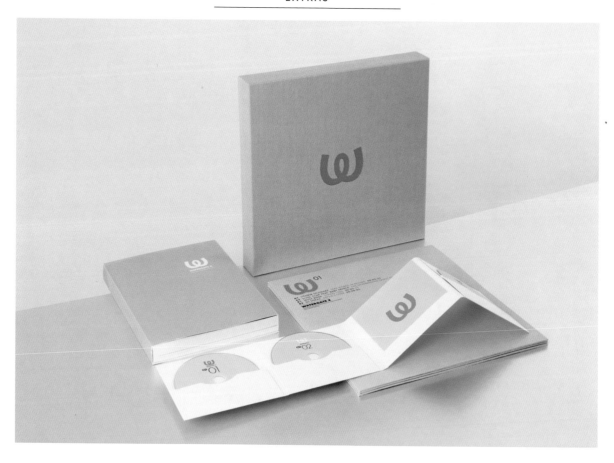

Watergate
X

Design
2 CDs
3 12" vinyl records
Booklet
DVD
Embossing
Exposed binding
Foil stamping
Lift-off-lid box
Linen
Matt varnish
Paperback book
Poster
Voucher
Edition of 1,000

Watergate is a Berlin nightclub, a record label and a DJ agency. Released as part of its tenth anniversary celebrations, the *X* limited-edition box set is intended to showcase the most important aspect of Watergate: the music.
—

PUBLISHER *Watergate Records, Germany*
ART DIRECTION & DESIGN *Alexander Seeberg-Elverfeldt*
PHOTOGRAPHY *Kai Jakob*
ILLUSTRATION *DAG*
DATE *2012*

Bill Bruford
The Autobiography

++++++++++++++

Specifications
2 art prints
2 10" vinyl records
10" custom-made cymbal
Black faux suede
Blind embossing
Die cutting
Foil blocking
Hand-bound
Hand feathering
Hand-numbered
Hand-signed
Hardback book
Laser etching
Red vinyl-coated paper
Screen printing
Slip case
Solander box
Edition of 25

Known as the godfather of progressive-rock drumming, Bill Bruford began his professional musical career in 1968. *The Autobiography* is his memoir of life at the heart of prog rock, art rock and modern jazz. Limited to twenty-five copies, this deluxe edition of the book includes a custom-made splash cymbal, forged from a bronze developed specifically for cymbals.

—

PUBLISHER *Foruli, UK*
ART DIRECTION & DESIGN *Andy Vella*
PHOTOGRAPHY *Andy Vella*
ILLUSTRATION *Andy Vella*
PRODUCTION *Whitmont Press, Paiste*
YEAR *2012*

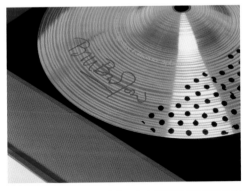

Oliver Jeffers
Neither Here Nor There

+++++++++++++

Specifications
4 giclee prints
Adhesive gilding
Embossing
Handmade walnut box
Hand-numbered
Hand-signed
Hardback book
Screen print
Edition of 30

Perhaps best known as the creator of award-winning picture books for children, New York-based Oliver Jeffers also maintains a successful career as a fine artist. *Neither Here Nor There* reveals the full range of Jeffers's work, from painting and collage to installations and more collaborative projects.

According to Jeffers, the special edition 'was the perfect opportunity to produce a beautiful package to accompany the book'. Wood was chosen for the box as it was a material that suited Jeffers's aesthetic. 'I have several friends here in New York who work with wood,' he explains, 'and it's hard not to get excited about seeing some of the hardwoods that come through their workshops. Once we'd decided on the design, we looked at many different options to get the box we wanted.'

Included with the book are various prints of some of the featured works, Jeffers's favourites, in fact. 'With the prints, we really wanted to produce something special', says Jeffers. 'The art chosen for the screen print went through several levels of re-working before we agreed on the final design. [Printmaker] Mark Herschede gave us loads of options, including special inks to make the edition even more elaborate. We finally agreed on screen-printing adhesive and applying gilding by hand. The print is pretty special.'
—

PUBLISHER *Gestalten, Germany*
ART DIRECTION *Oliver Jeffers, Richard Seabrook*
DESIGN *Conor & David*
ILLUSTRATION *Oliver Jeffers*
PRODUCTION *Blackburn Woodworking, Mark Herschede (Haven Press), Axelle Fine Arts*
DATE *2012*

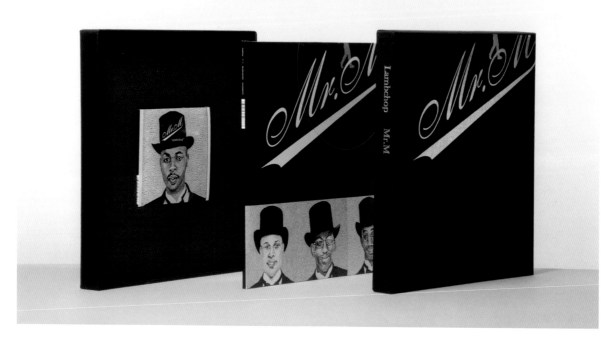

Lambchop
Mr. M

| | | | | | | | | | | | | | | | | | | | | | | | | | | | | |

Specifications
2 12" vinyl records
3-panel digipak
11 art prints
Artist portrait
Black linen
Booklet
CD
DVD
Embossing
Envelope
Foil stamping
Gatefold sleeve
Hand-signed letter
Lift-off-lid box
Silver and gold foil
Uncoated board
Edition of 200

The artwork for *Mr. M*, Lambchop's eleventh studio album, was created by Kurt Wagner, singer, songwriter and guitarist for the American alt-country band. Wagner had first turned to painting to deal with the premature death of American singer-songwriter Vic Chesnutt, for whom Lambchop had acted as a backing band. This limited-edition version of *Mr. M* – German record label City Slang's first-ever box set – includes a selection of prints of Wagner's art, together with a letter signed by Wagner.
—

PUBLISHER *City Slang, Germany*
DESIGN *New Formalists*
PHOTOGRAPHY *Bill Steber*
ARTWORK *Kurt Wagner*
DATE *2012*

Paul & Linda McCartney
RAM

++++++++++++++++

Specifications
2 paperback books
2 string-tie envelopes
4 CDs
Die cutting
DVD
Foil blocking
Hessian book cloth
Photographic prints
Scrapbook insert
Screen printing
Solander box
Stochastic printing

Originally released in 1971, *RAM* was the first album in the Paul McCartney Archive Collection to receive the super-deluxe treatment. After many rounds of experimentation, a clamshell format was selected for the box. This contains a rich variety of material designed to evoke the free-spirited nature of the early 1970s. Among the items included is a paperback book with a screen-printed cover, a set of photographic prints, a scrapbook containing unseen photography and drawings, facsimiles of handwritten lyrics, and a mini photo book featuring all the sheep photographed during the original cover shoot. In 2013 the project was nominated for two separate Grammy Awards: Best Historical Album, and Best Boxed or Special Limited Edition Package.
—

PUBLISHER *MPL/Concord/Universal Music, UK*
ART DIRECTION & DESIGN *Yes*
CREATIVE CONSULTANT *Roger Huggett*
PHOTOGRAPHY *Linda McCartney*
ORIGINAL ARTWORK *Paul McCartney*
PRINT PRODUCTION *Brian Schuman*
PRODUCTION *MPL*
DATE *2012*

Rachel Whiteread
Mike and the Modelmakers

Specifications
Artist's bookplate
Embossing
Embroidery
Hand-numbered
Hand-signed
Hardback book
Linen
Screen printing
Solander box
Woven cloth
Zinc cast of Matchbox toy
Edition of 40

When asked to participate in the series 'Edition Ex Libris' (see page 242), British artist Rachel Whiteread selected a children's book about the manufacture of Matchbox toys: *Mike and the Modelmakers* (1970), by Czech author and illustrator Miroslav Sasek. 'I chose this book', she explains, 'because it is related to where I live and how I work. My old studio was next to the site of the original Matchbox factory [in Hackney, east London]. A lot of these industrial buildings were demolished for the 2012 Olympics. I found an original copy of the book in a junk shop in the late 1980s. It seemed like a fitting tribute to those old buildings, to Sasek, and to those great Matchbox cars. I was happy to give it a new lease of life.' The collector's edition includes a Matchbox cement mixer cast in zinc – a subtle reference to the artist's casting of buildings in cement – and a cloth for cleaning machinery, embroidered with the artist's name and edition details.

—

PUBLISHER *Salon Verlag & Edition, Germany*
DESIGN *Rachel Whiteread*
ILLUSTRATION *Miroslav Sasek*
DATE *2008*

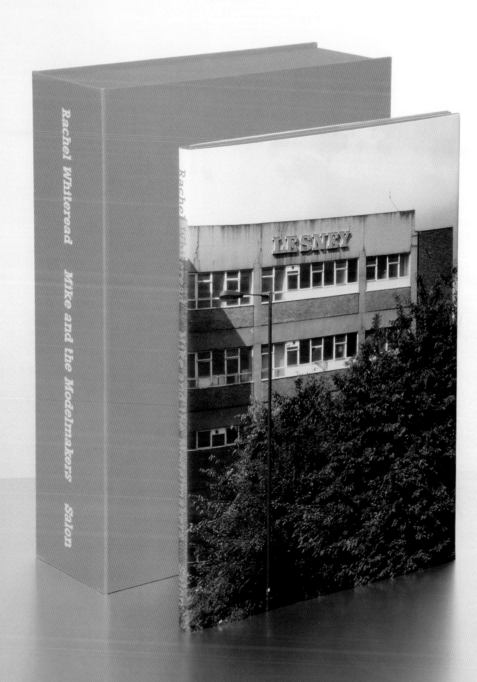

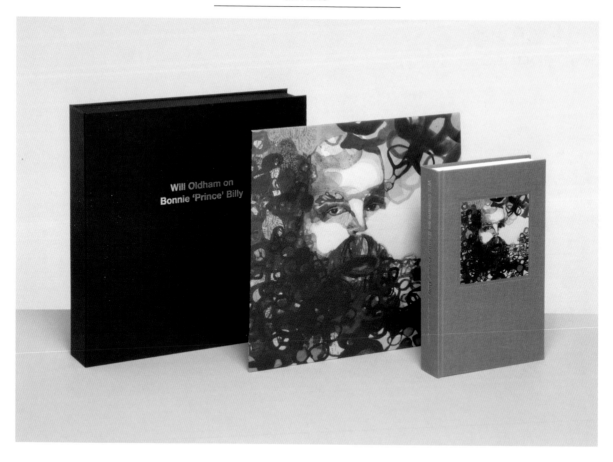

Will Oldham
Will Oldham on Bonnie 'Prince' Billy

Specifications
2 10" vinyl records
Foil blocking
Hand-numbered
Hand-signed
Hardback book
Silver foil
Solander box
Tipped-in illustration
Edition of 300

Will Oldham, aka Bonnie 'Prince' Billy, is an American singer-songwriter and actor. In *Will Oldham on ...*, he discusses his highly individualistic approach to music making and the music industry in a series of conversations with long-time friend and associate Alan Licht. This limited-edition box set includes two 10" records of exclusive material recorded by Oldham in January 2012.

—

PUBLISHER *Faber and Faber, UK*
DESIGN *Eleanor Crow (Faber and Faber)*
PRODUCTION *Jack Murphy (Faber and Faber)*
ILLUSTRATION *Becky Blair*
DATE *2012*

Big Cosmos
Illuminance

+++++++++++++

Specifications
Booklet
Finishing wax
Lacquer
Laser cutting
Poster
Rubber
Screen printing
String
USB wristband
Wood stain
Wooden box
Edition of 50

Illuminance is the debut EP by London-based five-piece Big Cosmos. According to the band, the limited-edition box set represents 'a multimedia artwork that is both physical and digital'. Contained in the home-made, laser-cut box are the EP on a USB wristband, a screen-printed poster and a lyric booklet. The EP was also released on a very limited number of pink cassette tapes.

—

PUBLISHER *Blessing Force, UK*
DESIGN *Claire Bailey*
PRODUCTION *Claire Bailey,*
Art Quarters Press
DATE *2013*

Pachanga Boys
We Are Really Sorry

+++++++++++++

Specifications
2 12" vinyl records
30-colour wax crayon set
African wenge wood
Booklet
CD
Colouring book
Dried flowers
DVD
Engraving
Hand stamping
Multi-compartment box
Music box
Organic alpaca wool
Organic straw
Pine
Postcard
Screen printing
Silver plate
Woollen guacamole
Woollen tortilla chip
Edition of 125

After founding their own record label in 2011, DJ duo Aksel Schaufler and Mauricio Rebolledo, aka the Pachanga Boys, soon became known for their unusual limited-edition EPs. When it came to *We Are Really Sorry*, their debut album, the intention was once again to produce something unique. Having amassed enough material for a road movie and a booklet, based on film and photographs of the album's making, the duo began to wonder what other items they could include in a limited-edition box set. The answer soon became clear: whatever they would want to find in a special edition.

Assembled by hand, the 'Hippie Dance Atelier Super Limited Collector's Edition' contains an eclectic mix of extras. Of particular note are a 'psychedelic' colouring book featuring wild animals, naked ladies and avocado spaceships; a set of Pachanga-branded crayons; a hand-knitted *totopo* (tortilla chip) brooch, 'served' on wool guacamole; a Paris-made music box that plays 'Fiesta Forever', the Pachanga Boys' first release; and a postcard bearing their motto, 'Love Power Pachanga', to send to 'the one you love'.

The last piece of the package is the box itself. Made from pine, and filled with organic straw, the box is decorated on its lid with a screen-printed graphic inspired by the album's artwork. The interior is divided into a number of compartments. These are designed to hold not only the various items listed above, but also the owner's own possessions and any future gifts from the Pachanga Boys.
—

PUBLISHER *Hippie Dance Atelier, Mexico/ Germany/France*
ART DIRECTION & DESIGN *Aksel Schaufler, Mauricio Rebolledo*
DATE *2012*

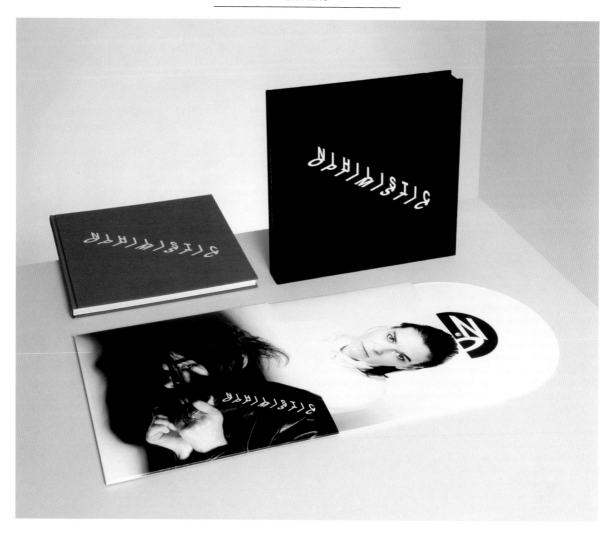

Tim Noble & Sue Webster
Nihilistic Optimistic

+++++++++++++

Specifications
10" vinyl record
Book cloth
Hand-numbered
Hand-signed
Hardback book
Solander box
Edition of 200

Staged in 2012 at the Blain Southern gallery in London, *Nihilistic Optimistic* was British artist duo Tim Noble and Sue Webster's first major solo exhibition in the capital since 2006. What initially began as a project to design a catalogue soon grew into something larger: a clamshell box containing the book and a record by the artists.

Developed from a sketch by Noble and Webster, the 'Nihilistic Optimistic' logo echoes the shadow sculptures from the exhibition: collections of 'rubbish' that, when lit from a certain angle, cast shadows that resemble the outlines of the artists themselves. The decision to use a largely monochrome palette throughout reflects not only the minimalism of the project's title but also these same sculptures, which, on an elementary level, are about light and dark.

—
PUBLISHER *Blain Southern/The Vinyl Factory, UK*
DESIGN *Damon Murray, Stephen Sorrell (FUEL)*
PHOTOGRAPHY *Dennis Morris*
PRODUCTION *MM Artbook Printing & Repro, The Vinyl Factory*
DATE *2012*

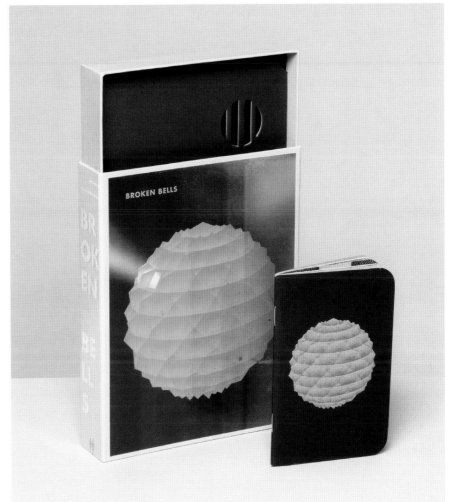

Specifications
2 postcards
CD
Glow-in-the-dark ink
Matt lamination
Moleskin-style notebook
Music box
Poster
Spot UV varnish
Stickers

When removed from its outer sleeve, this limited-edition music-box version of the debut album by Broken Bells – a collaboration between Brian Burton, aka Danger Mouse, and James Mercer from The Shins – plays a song recorded especially for the project. Its designer, Jacob Escobedo, wanted the box to feel like an old science fiction book. In addition to the album on CD, the box includes a sheet of glow-in-the-dark stickers, a poster and a forty-five-page Moleskin-style notebook filled with geometric shapes suspended above pink landscapes.

—

PUBLISHER *Columbia Records, USA*
ART DIRECTION & DESIGN *Jacob Escobedo*
ILLUSTRATION *Jacob Escobedo*
PHOTOGRAPHY *Frank W. Ockenfels III*
DATE *2010*

Broken Bells
Broken Bells

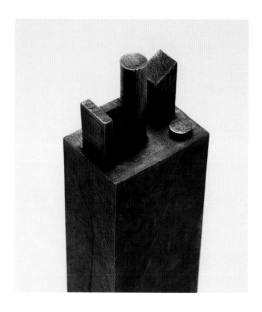

Matthew Dear
Black City

Specifications
Bonded aluminium
Gunmetal patina
Hand-cast
Inscription
Totem with download code
Edition of 100

In 2010, with digital downloads on the rise, American record label Ghostly International decided to explore the relationship between the intangible nature of MP3s and the physical media on which music has traditionally been supplied. Inspired by the lyrics of American musician Matthew Dear's album *Black City*, the label commissioned New York-based Boym Partners to craft an object that would represent the album abstractly and carry a code for accessing the digital version of the album online.

The result was Totem, a constructivist-like piece that from some angles resembles a building and from others a key. The designers chose to work with bonded aluminium, which is more cost-effective than solid metal and would keep shipping costs to a minimum. Each piece was hand-cast and hand-finished by third-generation craftsmen working locally in Queens, New York, and was inscribed on the bottom with the download code. Imperfections in the production process make each totem unique.
—

PUBLISHER *Ghostly International, USA*
ART DIRECTION *Will Calcutt*
DESIGN *Boym Partners*
YEAR *2010*

Vogue Nederland
Issue 1

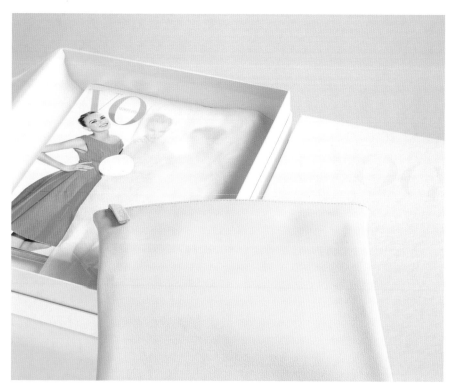

Specifications
Cover print
Drawstring bag
Embossing
Foil blocking
Gold zip
Handmade box
Hand-numbered
Hand-signed
Leather pouch
Magazine
Matt lamination
White blotting paper
Wool felt
Edition of 100

The white-and-grey palette used for this limited-edition gift box – released to mark the first edition of *Vogue Nederland* – was intended to create a minimalist aesthetic evoking 'newness'. The materials were selected for their luxurious feel, as were special papers and other small details, all of which were designed to create subtle differences in tactility. Accompanied by a personal note from the editor-in-chief of *Vogue Nederland*, Karin Swerink, the gift box was presented to such Dutch celebrities as the fashion designers Viktor & Rolf and the model Doutzen Kroes.

—

PUBLISHER *G&J Uitgevers, The Netherlands*
CREATIVE DIRECTION *Jochem Leegstra (...,staat creative agency)*
ART DIRECTION *Jamie Mitchell*
DESIGN *...,staat, Kim Keogh, Solar Initiative*
PHOTOGRAPHY *Marc de Groot*
PRODUCTION *Rood & Groen, Drukkerij WC den Ouden*
DATE *2012*

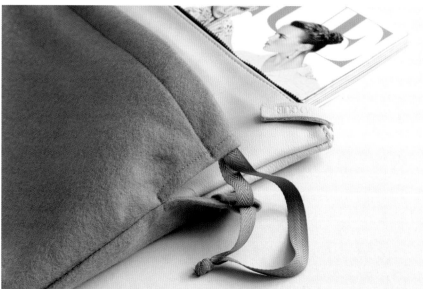

Neon Trees
Picture Show

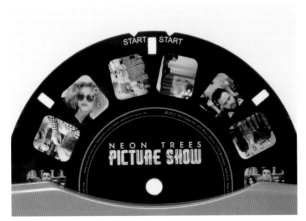

Specifications
16 custom film posters
3D plastic View-Master
Booklet
CD
View-Master reel

For *Picture Show*, the second album by American alternative rock band Neon Trees, the designers were given a very specific brief: to create a fictional female character who always wears red heart-shaped sunglasses, and to design a film poster for every song on the album. A key component of the deluxe box set is a 3D View-Master complete with a reel of exclusive images from the film-poster photo shoot.

—

PUBLISHER *Island Def Jam Music Group, USA*
CREATIVE DIRECTION *Todd Russell, Tyler Glenn, Autumn de Wilde*
ART DIRECTION & DESIGN *Todd Russell, Steve DeFino*
PHOTOGRAPHY *Autumn de Wilde*
DATE *2012*

Yayoi Kusama
Lewis Carroll's Alice's Adventures in Wonderland

Specifications
Acrylic
Art print
Book cloth
Canvas
Embossing
Foil blocking
Hand-numbered
Hand-signed
Hardback book
Lift-off-lid box
Passepartout frames
Photographic print
Portfolio
Screen-print glaze
Screen printing
Edition of 111

Yayoi Kusama's illustrated version of *Alice's Adventures in Wonderland* was published by Penguin Classics; this special edition was a collaboration between Penguin and Louis Vuitton. The overall design is in keeping with the various products that the Japanese artist and writer has designed for the luxury brand. The large difference in size between the box (76 × 53 cm/30 × 20⅞ in.) and the book alludes to the changes in scale in the *Alice* story. Also included in the box is a print of a self-portrait by Kusama, who has described herself as 'the modern Alice in Wonderland'.
—

PUBLISHER *Penguin Classics, UK*
ART DIRECTION & DESIGN
Stefanie Posavec
EDITOR *Alexis Kirschbaum*
ILLUSTRATION *Yayoi Kusama*
PRODUCTION *Graphicom, Coriander Studio, James Blackman (Penguin Books), Metro Imaging*
DATE *2012*

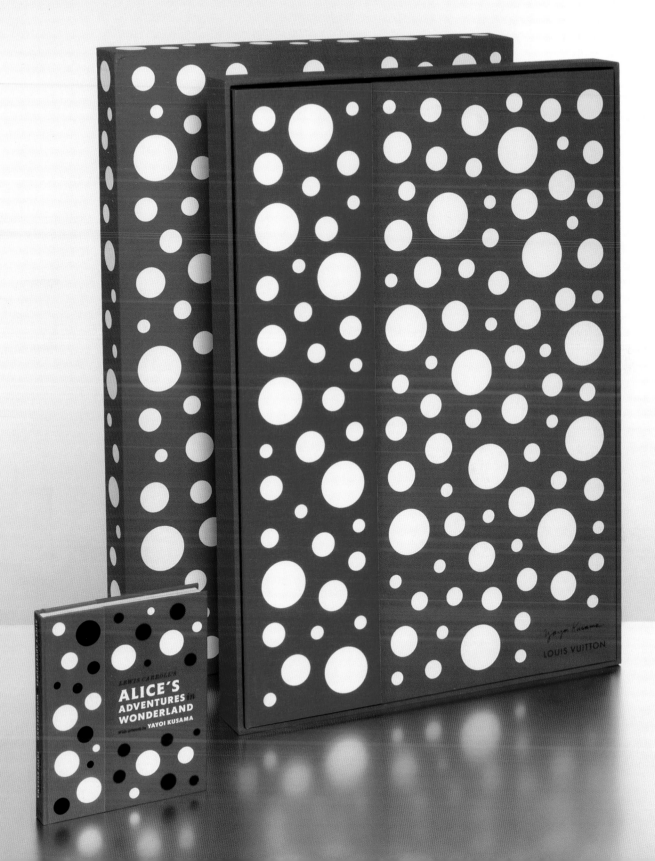

Art Direction & Design

...,staat creative agency
www.staatamsterdam.nl

A Practice for Everyday Life
www.apracticeforeverydaylife.com

Alexander Seeberg-Elverfeldt
www.bureau-aeiou.com

Andrew Sloat
www.andrewsloat.com

Andy Hau
www.andyhau.com

Andy Vella Design
www.velladesign.com

Anneka Beatty
www.annekabeatty.ch

Atlantique Studio
www.atlantiquestudio.com

Bibliothèque
www.bibliothequedesign.com

Blaine Fontana
www.thefontanastudios.com

Bruno Margreth
www.brunomargreth.ch

Bruno Stucchi
www.dinamomilano.com

Caroline Robert
www.caroline-robert.com

Christian Schienerl
www.schienerl.com

Conor & David
www.conoranddavid.com

Coralie Bickford-Smith
www.cb-smith.com

Daniel Eatock
www.eatock.com

Daniela Meloni
www.danielameloni.com

David Carson
www.davidcarsondesign.com

David J. Woodruff
www.davidjwoodruff.com

Davy Evans
www.davyevans.co.uk

Distant Station Ltd.
www.distantstation.com

Double Standards
www.doublestandards.net

FUEL
www.fuel-design.com

Gabriele F. Götz
www.ambulantdesign.nl

Gareth White
www.newfuturegraphic.co.uk

George Salisbury
www.delocreative.com

Give Up Art
www.giveupart.com

Hanna Zeckau
www.kiosk-royal.com

Hans Gremmen
www.hansgremmen.nl

Henrik Kubel
www.a2swhk.co.uk

Higher and Higher
www.higherandhigher.com

Hiroshi Tanabe
www.hiroshitanabe.com

Hort
www.hort.org.uk

Intro
www.intro-uk.com

Irma Boom
www.irmaboom.nl

Jacob Escobedo
www.jacobescobedo.com

Jamie Mitchell
www.jamiemitchell.com.au

Jeff Jank
www.jeffjank.com

Jessica Hische
www.jessicahische.is

Joe Zeff Design
www.joezeffdesign.com

John Gall
www.johngalldesign.com

John Morgan
www.morganstudio.co.uk

Jon Abbott
www.jon-abbott.com

Jon Wiese
www.john-wiese.com

Jonathan Barnbrook
www.barnbrook.net

Jonathan Mangelinckx
www.mangelinckx.com

Kummer & Herrman
www.kummer-herrman.nl

Lafont London
www.lafont.ch

Laurent Fétis
www.laurentfetis.com

Lawrence Azerrad
www.laddesign.net

Leif Podhajsky
www.leifpodhajsky.com

Leonidas Ikonomou
www.leonidasikonomou.com

Lucas Maassen
www.lucasmaassen.nl

Magdalena Czarnecki
www.tjaneski.com

Magma Brand Design
www.magmabranddesign.de

Malcolm Garrett
www.images.co.uk

Marc Bessant
www.marcbessant.com

Matt Taylor
www.varnishstudio.com

Melanie Mues
www.muesdesign.com

Michael Cina
www.michaelcinaassociates.com

M/M (Paris)
www.mmparis.com

Nick Robertson
www.wordsalad.co.uk

Oblivious Artefacts
www.obliviousartefacts.com

Oscar & Ewan
www.oscarandewan.se

Other Means
www.othermeans.us

Peter and Paul
www.peterandpaul.co.uk

Pfadfinderei
www.pfadfinderei.com

Philipp Hubert
www.visiotypen.com

Quentin Newark
www.atelierworks.co.uk

Raw Color
www.rawcolor.nl

reflexblue
www.reflexblue.co.uk

Sam Baron
www.sambaron.fr

Sense/Net
www.sense-net.net

Simon Slater
www.behance.net/laki139

Smog Design Inc.
www.smogdesign.com

Stefan Sagmeister
www.sagmeisterwalsh.com

Stefanie Posavec
www.itsbeenreal.co.uk

Stephen Serrato
www.sserrato.info

Steve DeFino
www.stevedefino.com

Studio Frith
www.studiofrith.com

Tappin Gofton
www.tappingofton.com

TBWA
www.tbwa.se

The Curved House
www.thecurvedhouse.com

The Designers Republic
www.thedesignersrepublic.com

Todd Russell
www.todd-russell.com

Tom Hingston Studio
www.hingston.net

Tom Skipp
www.tomskipp.com

Torsten Posselt
www.feld.is

Trevor Jackson
www.trevor-jackson.com

Typoretum
www.typoretum.co.uk

Vaughan Oliver (V23)
www.v23.biz

Vince Frost
www.frostdesign.com.au

Yes
www.yesstudio.co.uk

Zwölf
www.zwoelf.hu

Books & Magazines

Annual Magazine
www.annualartmagazine.com
Aperture Foundation
www.aperture.org
Aura
www.laki139.com
Blain Southern
www.blainsouthern.com
Book Works
www.bookworks.org.uk
Browns Editions
www.brownseditions.com
Buchhandlung Walther König
www.buchhandlung-walther-koenig.de
Colors
www.colorsmagazine.com
Departure
www.departure.at
Der Greif
www.dergreif-online.de
Dewi Lewis Publishing
www.dewilewispublishing.com
Die Schachtel
www.dieschachtel.com
DoPe Press
www.dopepress.fr
Edition Dino Simonett
www.simonett.com
Erasmus Publishing
www.jamesjennifergeorgina.com
Foruli
www.foruli.co.uk
Four Corners
www.fourcornersbooks.co.uk
FUEL Publishing
www.fuel-design.com/publishing
Fw: Publishers
www.fw-photography.nl
Harper's Bazaar
www.harpersbazaar.co.uk
Harvill Secker
www.vintage-books.co.uk/about-us/harvill-secker
Hatje Cantz Verlag
www.hatjecantz.de
Lehmann Maupin
www.lehmannmaupin.com
Little Brown Mushroom
www.littlebrownmushroom.com
Mizuma Art Gallery
www.mizuma-art.co.jp

mono.kultur
www.mono-kultur.com
Nieves
www.nieves.ch
Nobody Books
www.nobodybooks.com
Novum
www.novumnet.de
Other Criteria
www.othercriteria.com
Paragon Press
www.paragonpress.co.uk
Penguin Books UK
www.penguin.co.uk
Penguin Books USA
www.us.penguingroup.com
PogoBooks Verlag
www.pogobooks.de
Qompendium Print Publication
www.qompendium.com
Raking Leaves
www.rakingleaves.org
Reel Art Press
www.reelartpress.com
RVB Books
www.rvb-books.com
Salon Verlag & Edition
www.salon-verlag.de
Seigensha Art Publishing
www.seigensha.com
Slanted
www.slanted.de
Steidl
www.steidl.de
Tara Books
www.tarabooks.com
TASCHEN
www.taschen.com
Tate Publishing
www.tate.org.uk
The Folio Society
www.foliosociety.com
The Hunger
www.hungertv.com
The Moth House
www.themothhouse.com
The Sochi Project
www.thesochiproject.org
Thomas Dane Gallery
www.thomasdanegallery.com
Three Star Books
www.threestarbooks.com

V&A Publishing
www.vam.ac.uk
VdH Books
www.vdhbooks.com
Very Nearly Almost
www.verynearlyalmost.com
Vintage Books
www.vintage-books.co.uk
Visi
www.visi.co.za
Vogue Nederland
www.vogue.nl
Wallpaper*
www.wallpaper.com
Zabludowicz Collection
www.zabludowiczcollection.com
ZERO+ Publishing
www.zeropluspublishing.com

Illustration & Art

Aiko Miyanaga
www.aiko-m.com
Andy Holden
www.andyholdenartist.com
Anthony Burrill
www.anthonyburrill.com
Autumn de Wilde
www.autumndewilde.com
B+
www.mochilla.com
Becky Blair
www.beckyblairartist.co.uk
Bohyun Yoon
www.bohyunyoon.com
Carson Ellis
www.carsonellis.com
Charles Wilkin
www.charlesscottwilkin.com
Daisy de Villeneuve
www.daisydevilleneuve.com
Despotica
www.despotica.com
Dinos Chapman
www.jakeanddinoschapman.com
Fernando Mastrangelo
www.fernandomastrangelo.com
Gregory Euclide
www.gregoryeuclide.com
Gustavo Eandi
www.disciplina.gustavoeandi.com
Harry Brockway
www.harrybrockway.com
HelloVon
www.hellovon.com
Herr Müller
www.183off.com
Human Connectome Project
www.humanconnectomeproject.org
Ian Stevenson
www.ianstevenson.co.uk
Ian Wright
www.mrianwright.co.uk
Isabel Samaras
www.isabelsamaras.com
James Joyce
www.jamesjoyce.co.uk
Jillian Tamaki
www.jilliantamaki.com
John Solimine
www.spikepress.com
Kam Tang
www.kamtang.co.uk

Music

Kid Acne
www.kidacne.com

Kottie Paloma
www.kottiepaloma.com

Kundalini Arts
www.kundaliniarts.co.uk

Langdon Graves
www.langdongraves.com

Liam Gillick
www.liamgillick.info

Martin Creed
www.martincreed.com

Miroslav Sasek
www.miroslavsasek.com

Neil Krug
www.neilkrug.com

Oliver Jeffers
www.oliverjeffers.com

Paris
www.paris1974.com

Quentin Jones
www.quentinjones.info

Rob Ryan
www.robryanstudio.com

Rory McCartney
www.rorymccartney.com

Sam Winston
www.samwinston.com

Stanley Donwood
www.slowlydownward.com

Stéphanie Solinas
www.stephaniesolinas.com

Stephen Raw
www.stephenraw.com

Steven Wilson
www.stevenwilsonstudio.com

Supermundane
www.supermundane.com

Tine Klink
www.tineklink.de

Tracey Emin
www.traceyeminstudio.com

Vincent Morisset
www.vincentmorisset.com

WassinkLundgren
www.wassinklundgren.com

Wolfgang Voigt
www.wolfgang-voigt.com

Woody Veneman
www.woodyveneman.nl

Yayoi Kusama
www.yayoi-kusama.jp

4AD
www.4ad.com

12K
www.12k.com

100% Records
www.100-percent.co.uk

Alt Vinyl
www.altvinyl.com

Artist in Residence
www.ainr.com

Attenuation Circuit
www.attenuationcircuit.wix.com/
attenuation-circuit

Big Brother Recordings Ltd
www.rkid003.blogspot.co.uk

Bleep
www.bleep.com

Blessing Force
www.blessingforce.com

BMG
www.bmg.com

Bokhari Records
www.bokharirecords.com

Budde Music
www.buddemusic.de

Capitol Records
www.capitolrecords.com

Catskills Records
www.catskillsrecords.com

City Slang
www.cityslang.com

Columbia Records
www.columbiarecords.com

Concord Music Group
www.concordmusicgroup.com

Coppice
www.futurevessel.com

Dangerbird Records
www.dangerbirdrecords.com

dBpm Records
www.dbpmrecords.com

Death Waltz Records
www.deathwaltzrecording
company.com

D/struct
www.d-struct.nl

Full Psycho Records
www.fullpsychorecords.com

Ghostly International
www.ghostly.com

Giant Drag
www.anniehardy.bandcamp.com

Gift of the Gab Records
www.giftofthegabrecords.com

Green United Music
www.greenunitedmusic.com

Greenpot Bluepot
www.greenpotbluepot.tumblr.com

Inner Ear Records
www.inner-ear.gr

Invisible Spies Records
www.invisiblespiesrecords.
wordpress.com

Island Def Jam Group
www.islanddefjam.com

Island Records
www.islandrecords.co.uk

Joyful Noise Recordings
www.joyfulnoiserecordings.com

Kompakt
www.kompakt.fm

Lex Records
www.lexprojects.com

Lost Toys Records
www.losttoysrecords.com

Macklemore & Ryan Lewis
www.macklemore.com

Matador Records
www.matadorrecords.com

Meowtain
www.meowtain.bandcamp.com

Merge Records
www.mergerecords.com

Moldover
www.moldover.com

Monkeytown Records
www.monkeytownrecords.com

MPL Communications
www.mplcommunications.com

Mute
www.mute.com

Ninja Tune
www.ninjatune.net

One Little Indian Records
www.indian.co.uk

Pachanga Boys
www.kompakt.fm/artists/
pachanga_boys

Parlophone
www.parlophone.co.uk

Piaptk Recordings
www.piaptk.limitedrun.com

Profan
www.kompakt.fm/labels/profan

Project Bootleg
www.cargocollective.com/
manuelandmax

Quadrofoon Records
www.quadrofoon.com

Radiohead
www.radiohead.com

Random Noize Musick
www.randomnoizemusick.com

Real World
www.realworld.co.uk

Rekids
www.rekids.com

Rune Grammofon
www.runegrammofon.com

Shout Out Louds
www.shoutoutlouds.com

Sigur Rós
www.sigur-ros.co.uk

Spoon Records
www.spoonrecords.com

SPV Records
www.spv.de

Stroboscopic Artefacts
www.stroboscopicartefacts.com

Systematic Records
www.systematic-recordings.com

Taiga Records
www.taigarecords.com

The Flaming Lips
www.flaminglips.com

Time Released Sound
www.timereleasedsound.com

Universal Music Group
www.universalmusic.com

Unoiki
www.unoiki.net

Vlek
www.vlek.tumblr.com

Warner Bros. Records
www.warnerbrosrecords.com

Warner/Chappell
www.warnerchappell.co.uk

Warp
www.warp.net

Watergate
www.water-gate.de

XL Recordings
www.xlrecordings.com

Photography

Alec Soth
www.alecsoth.com
Bene Brandhofer
www.beneb.de
Bill Steber
www.steberphoto.com
Bruce Gilden
www.brucegilden.com
Dan Holdsworth
www.danholdsworth.com
Danny Clinch
www.dannyclinch.com
Dennis Morris
www.dennismorris.com
Dominique Issermann
www.dominiqueissermann.com
Donald Milne
www.donaldmilne.com
Edgar Martins
www.edgarmartins.com
Gavin Bond
www.gavinbondphotography.com
Giles Revell
www.gilesrevell.com
Greg Watermann
www.gregwatermann.com
Heidi de Gier
www.heididegier.nl
Hugo Glendinning
www.hugoglendinning.com
Inez van Lamsweerde &
Vinoodh Matadin
www.inezandvinoodh.com
Kevin Westenberg
www.kevinwestenberg.com
Leon Kirchlechner
www.leonkirchlechner.com
Lukas Wassmann
www.lukaswassmann.com
Marc de Groot
www.marcdegroot.co.uk
Mario Testino
www.mariotestino.com
Matthias Lohscheidt
www.mlohscheidt.de
Melvin Galapon
www.mynameismelvin.co.uk
Michael Kohls
www.michaelkohls.com
Mitch Jenkins
www.mitchjenkins.com
Nadav Kander
www.nadavkander.com

Rankin
www.rankin.co.uk
Richard Mosse
www.richardmosse.com
Rob Hornstra
www.borotov.nl
Sandra Steh
www.steh.de
Shaun Bloodworth
www.shaunbloodworth.com
Simon Karlstetter
www.simonkarlstetter.de
Simon Larbalestier
www.simon-larbalestier.co.uk
Simon Norfolk
www.simonnorfolk.com
Stephen Gill
www.stephengill.co.uk
Sterling Andrews
www.sterlingandrews.com
Steve Gschmeissner
www.theworldcloseup.com
Thomas Mailaender
www.thomasmailaender.com
Tim Noble & Sue Webster
www.timnobleandsuewebster.com
Todd Hido
www.toddhido.com
Will Calcutt
www.willcalcutt.com
Wolfgang Tillmans
www.tillmans.co.uk

Print & Production

Artomatic
www.artomatic.co.uk
Badger Press
www.badgerpress.org
Blackburn Woodworking
www.blackburnwoodworking.com
Boekbinderij Van Waarden
www.boekbinderijvanwaarden.nl
Boym Partners
www.boym.com
Clear Sound & Vision
www.clearsoundandvision.com
Coriander Studio
www.corianderstudio.com
D'Andrea Graphics
www.dandreagraphics.com
David A. Carter
www.popupbooks.com
Deep Wood Workshop
www.deepwoodworkshop.com
Derek Lawson
www.giantgummybears.com
Disc Solutions
www.discsolutions.co.uk
Dr. Cantz'sche Druckerei
www.cantz.de
Drukkerij Raddraaier
www.raddraaier.nl
E&B Engelhardt und Bauer
www.ebdruck.de
GGP Media
www.ggp-media.de
Gold Phoenix PCB
www.goldphoenixpcb.com
Gruber Druck und Medien
www.gruber-druck.de
Haven Press
www.havenpress.com
Holzhausen Druck GmbH
www.holzhausen.at
J. T. Sawyer & Co. Ltd
www.sawyersboxes.co.uk
Jade Bookbinding Studio
www.jadebookbindingstudio-
jadestudio.blogspot.co.uk
K2 Screen
www.k2screen.co.uk
Kobalt Label Services
www.kobaltmusic.com
Lecturis
www.lecturis.nl

Lenoirschuring
www.lenoirschuring.com
Martins the Printers
www.martins-the-printers.co.uk
MM Artbook Printing & Repro
www.mmartbookprinting.eu
Modo
www.modo.co.uk
Multi Packaging Solutions
www.multipkg.com
Napier Jones
www.napierjones.co.uk
Paiste
www.paiste.com
Paperlux
www.paperlux.com
Paragon Cutting Formes Ltd
www.paragoncfl.com
Paupers Press
www.pauperspublications.com
Pirates Press
www.piratespress.com
Progress Packaging
www.progresspackaging.co.uk
Schuster Custom Woodworking
www.schustercw.com
Something Else
www.somethingelse.gg
Spectrum Photo
www.spectrumphoto.co.uk
Stoughton Printing Co.
www.stoughtonprinting.com
The Fine Book Bindery
www.finebinding.co.uk
The Logan Press
www.theloganpress.co.uk
The Vinyl Factory
www.thevinylfactory.com
Think Tank Media
www.thinktankmedia.co.uk
VGKids
www.vgkids.com
White Duck Screen Print
www.whiteduckscreenprint.co.uk
Whitmont Press
www.whitmontpress.co.uk

About the Author

Stuart Tolley is an art director and graphic designer based in the United Kingdom. He has worked with some of the most prestigious magazines, lifestyle brands and book publishers of the last fifteen years. He began his career as a full-time designer at the award-winning *Sleazenation* magazine, later joining the *Independent on Saturday*'s magazine as the acting art director, and *Esquire UK* as a senior designer. He has worked with numerous editorial agencies, and has created bespoke magazines for high-profile lifestyle brands.

In 2009 Tolley founded Transmission, a creative communications agency and editorial consultancy. The studio works closely with publishing houses, arts institutes, non-profit organizations and lifestyle brands to art-direct bespoke magazines, books, editorial papers, book jackets and art exhibitions. The studio's work regularly features in the design press, visual-culture books and digital media, while its typographic screen prints have been exhibited in art galleries.

Credits

p. 86 © Tracey Emin. All rights reserved, DACS 2014

Art Direction & Design
Stuart Tolley (Transmission)
www.thisistransmission.com

Still-Life Photography
Ivan Jones *www.ivan-jones.co.uk*

Interviews
Matthew Lee

Portrait Photography
Emiliano Granado *www.emilianogranado.com*
Ivan Jones *www.ivan-jones.co.uk*
Daniel Shea *www.danielpshea.com*

Editor
Mark Ralph

Acknowledgments

This book is dedicated to Lynn Stevens, for her love and support over the last two years while I was busy working on this project. Sorry for missing all those sunny weekends away in Gomez. A massive 'thank you' goes out to Ivan Jones and Matthew Lee, for their generosity and creativity throughout. It was a pleasure working closely with both of them, on the photography and interviews respectively.

I would especially like to thank all the contributors for their participation, and for submitting the beautiful objects featured in the book. This project would not have been possible without their collaboration. Particular thanks also go to Sean Bidder, Scott Booker, Irma Boom, Derek Brown, Dinos Chapman, Wayne Coyne, Stanley Donwood, Robyn Katkhuda, Lehmann Maupin Gallery, Damon Murray, Stefan Sagmeister, Alec Soth and Carrie Thompson for their help with the exclusive interviews and portrait photography.

This has been an incredible journey, and I would like to thank Mark Ralph for editing the book, and the dedicated publishing team at Thames & Hudson – Tatiana Goodchild, Paul Hammond, Elisa Merino, Johanna Neurath, Andrew Sanigar and Amanda Vinnicombe – for believing in the concept and for their backing throughout.

In no particular order I would also like to thank Matt Ford from G. F. Smith, for supplying the Colorplan board and Peregrina Classics metallic-silver background paper; William Sadowski, for the loan of the Workflow photographic studio during the snowy winter months; Simon Kirkham, for helping me brainstorm the introduction; and Mark Swan and Stephen Elford, for letting me destroy the Hove studio.

Lastly, I would like to thank my family – Chris, Anita, Doug, Lou, Daisy, Ed Tolley and Giulia Priest – for their patience, as I have not been around much over the last two years.

First published in the United Kingdom in 2014 by Thames & Hudson Ltd, 181A High Holborn, London WC1V 7QX

Collector's Edition: Innovative Packaging and Graphics © 2014 Stuart Tolley

British Library Cataloguing-in-Publication Data
A catalogue record for this book is available from the British Library

ISBN 978-0-500-51757-4

Printed and bound in China by Everbest Printing Co. Ltd

To find out about all our publications, please visit **www.thamesandhudson.com**. There you can subscribe to our e-newsletter, browse or download our current catalogue, and buy any titles that are in print.